Risking It All

MY STUDENT

MY LOVER

MY STORY

# It All

## Heather E. Ingram

GREYSTONE BOOKS
Douglas & McIntyre Publishing Group
Vancouver/Toronto/New York

Greystone Books
A division of Douglas & McIntyre Ltd.
2323 Quebec Street, Suite 201
Vancouver, British Columbia
Canada V5T 4S7
www.greystonebooks.com

*National Library of Canada Cataloguing in Publication Data*
Ingram, Heather E. (Heather Elizabeth), 1969–
Risking it all: my student, my lover, my story / Heather E. Ingram.

ISBN 1-55054-980-4

1. Ingram, Heather E. (Heather Elizabeth), 1969– —Trials, litigation, etc.
2. Teachers—British Columbia—Sechelt—Biography. 3. Trials
(Child sexual abuse)—British Columbia. I. Title.
HV6626.54.C3I53 2003    364.15′554′0971131    C2003-910010-3

Editing by Nancy Flight
Jacket and text design by Peter Cocking
Jacket photograph by John Sherlock
Typesetting by Lynn O'Rourke
Printed and bound in Canada by Friesens
Distributed in the U.S. by Publishers Group West

We gratefully acknowledge the financial support of the Canada
Council for the Arts, the British Columbia Arts Council, and
the Government of Canada through the Book Publishing Industry
Development Program (BPIDP) for our publishing activities.

This book is dedicated to Troy, who taught me
everything I needed to learn about love, and without whom
my world would be an infinitely narrower place.


It is also dedicated to Lisa and Juli,
my sister and my soul sister, who taught me strength.

"I realized that once people are broken in certain ways,
they can't ever be fixed, and this is something
nobody ever tells you when you are young and it never fails
to surprise you as you grow older and you see the people
in your life break one by one. You wonder when
your turn is going to be, or if it's already happened."

DOUGLAS COUPLAND, *Life After God*


"Happiness is a solid, but joy is a liquid."

J.D. SALINGER, "De Daumier-Smith's Blue Period"
in *Nine Stories*

# Contents

# Preface

THIS BOOK BEGAN as a way to keep myself sane over the past four tumultuous
and often painful years. Much of it is taken from the journal I
kept after I began my relationship with "Troy." The impetus
to turn these journal ramblings into a book came from discussions with Troy and his mother and from the many people
who said, "You should write a book!"

The media's sensationalistic approach to our story was in-
furiating to me and seemed ridiculous to anybody who knew
us. Most of those who did know us as a couple, my friends and
Troy's, were entirely supportive of our relationship. I hope
that through these pages readers will come to know us, or at
least to see more than the one-dimensional figures portrayed
in the press and on TV. I hope that this account will make
clear how much remorse I feel and how hard it was to learn
the things I needed to learn. Never again will I believe that
doing well in school is education enough.

x   RISKING IT ALL

Some, but not all, of the names in the book have been changed to protect people who might be affected by some of the revelations. I don't want to hurt anybody more than I already have.

I am permanently indebted to Nancy Flight and Rob Sanders at Greystone Books for their patience and faith that the slim proposal I sent them could one day become a book worth reading. For their endless love and support and reading of many drafts, I thank Lisa Ingram, Juli Johnson, Kelly O'Neill, and Katherine Jeffcoatt. For their friendship even though they were "Troy's friends," I thank Brian Wilson, Andrew Anderson, Travis Tattrie, Jose Molina, Jessica Sangster, and all of the group in Sechelt—Jen, Tony, Jessa, Chrissy, Alicia, Angela, Tara, Tyrel, Rick, Dale, Jeremy, Christine, Jill, and more. I also thank my former students for their support, even when I was no longer their teacher.

Thank you to Gillian and Phyllis for caring for Seymour, and to Dona and Ric for giving me a place to show I could still contribute when I needed it the most. Thank you to the neighborhood of Grantham's Landing, especially the Allen family, for their warmth and acceptance.

For reading the whole thing from beginning to end even though he hates to read, I thank Stacy Baulne.

For her generosity to me and her undying love for her son, I thank Troy's mother.

Finally, thank you to my parents, Malcolm Ingram, Daphne Clancy, and Paul Clancy, for always being there, no matter what.

# Prologue

*A*s my sister's purple Honda crests the hill into Sechelt, I scan the parking lot of the courthouse for media. "Should I drive around, just to make sure?" Lisa asks.

Troy leans out the window. "Looks quiet," he says.

We park and walk unheeded up the stairs to the tiny courtroom above the lumber store. I have never been part of a courtroom proceeding before. My hands are sweating; my stomach muscles are clenched. Troy's hand grips mine as we climb the wooden stairs. I am wearing high heels, and I concentrate on not tripping on my long gray skirt. As we enter the courtroom, I lean into Troy's tall, calm shoulder.

We are scheduled for 11:00 A.M. Regular cases are dealt with in sequence, rather than at a specific time, but my crime is significant, possibly the most publicized case this small-town court has ever seen. The sheriff, a white-haired, heavyset man who appears to be borrowed from a Hollywood movie, leans over to whisper to us. "Your lawyer's ferry is late. The press are at the coffee shop down the street." His face is impassive but surprisingly kind. "Thank you," Lisa says. Our anonymity will be short lived.

A continuous wooden bench snakes around the edge of the drab waiting room. The threadbare carpet is hardly a color anymore. Outside the window, cracked asphalt stretches between the large piles of two-by-fours belonging to the lumber store underneath us. A man in a baseball cap drives a forklift across the yard.

The media arrive and gather at the front of the room. A woman with short dark hair and a black tailored suit lifts her head from her notebook and smiles tentatively at me. A tall, black, immaculately groomed man chats with another reporter, who sports jeans, a blue fleece vest, and a long-lensed camera. A television cameraman shifts his heavy video camera impatiently on his shoulder, while another reporter fiddles with a fat microphone. The sticker on the camera reads Global TV. I glance for reassurance at the sign in the waiting room that says No Photographs Allowed.

One by one, the reporters approach me. "Are you Heather Ingram?" The speaker is wearing a shapeless purple corduroy jumper and clogs—I guess that she is from the local paper. My lawyer has warned me repeatedly that I must not speak to the press, so I stifle my automatic reply and stare at her until she backs away.

Now the *Province* reporter moves in. "Will Troy speak to us?" He pats his vest for a pencil and looks at me.

I glance at Troy, this boy who is rapidly becoming a man,

who never bargained for this deal but is much stronger than I am. "You'll have to ask him," I say.

Troy turns to the reporter who has been pursuing us for the past five months. Yesterday, Sunday afternoon, he was trampling the flowers in Troy's mother's garden. Flashing and pointing his camera at her like a weapon, he forced her to retreat from the hydrangeas into her small house. Deadpan, Troy says to him, "Got a spare ten grand?" I almost laugh. Inside I rally a small cheer at his audacity, but on the outside I remain subdued and silent. Lisa gives my hand a squeeze. I am so amazed by my little sister. Since I lost my job in November, she has been like an army sergeant, forcing me to eat, aggressively shutting my front door on reporters, protecting me fiercely.

We are saved from the battle of silence by my lawyer, Bill. He hurries into the waiting room in his expensive navy suit, looking far too sophisticated for the surroundings. He is prosecuting British Columbia's former premier, for God's sake, and defending hockey player Marty McSorley. I want to apologize to him for the dingy courthouse, the late ferry, the lousy coffee shops, the amount of media my case has generated. With a lawyer's steely calm, he motions to us to follow him.

When Troy and I are seated in Crown counsel's small office, safely away from the reporters, Bill drops a bombshell. "I hate to do this to you so late in the game, but I've been thinking that . . . perhaps . . . you should plead *not guilty*," he says.

"What?" We are incredulous. After all, I admitted my relationship with Troy to my principal and to a colleague. Certainly I am guilty.

"Well," Bill says, "if Troy told you that he was eighteen, not seventeen, which he did, and if you had no reasonable grounds to doubt him, then . . ."

I am barely listening. I imagine Clifford Smith, the school district superintendent, and Vivian, my former friend and colleague, glaring from the witness box, telling the room what I have done. I imagine more newspaper articles, more agony for my family, more court proceedings. It has been five months since I was suspended from my job at Chatelech Secondary. I want more than anything to be done with this, to end the constant pain for me, Troy, and our families. In my mind I see my mother, her face tense but strong, and my father, crushed and disappointed, trying to find a way to still be proud of his daughter.

"The real question is," Bill says, "on June 9, 1999, did you wish him a happy eighteenth or happy nineteenth birthday?" This is crazy. How can my fate rest on something so insignificant? We began our affair in January of 1999, when Troy was five months shy of his eighteenth birthday. Troy looks at me intently. I know that he wants me to lie, to say that I really thought he was turning nineteen. He begs me with his eyes to lie, to take this small chance to save myself and my career. I consider this alternative only briefly, because I know I can't do it. The tiny bubble of hope that I feel rising to the surface breaks. I am exhausted; I can't face a trial; I can't live a hidden life anymore. Please, Troy, please understand.

Before this year I had never heard of the law. Section 153 of the Canadian Criminal Code, Sexual Exploitation of a Minor, says that any sexual contact, consensual or not, between a person under eighteen and a person in a position of direct authority is illegal. It is a relatively new law; Bill says that a decade ago I could not have been charged. The Crown does not have to prove I exploited Troy in any way. The fact that we had sexual contact is enough, and I have admitted this already.

"I knew," I say quietly. "I just didn't know that it mattered."

Bill looks at me, a mixture of respect and pity in his face, and shakes his head. "All right, then." He is all business. "Let's go."

Inside the courtroom the air is stale. When I was in high school, our class visited the majestic courtrooms of the Vancouver courthouse, where the imposing judges sat far away, at the front. A seedy contrast, this court is the size of a living room, with yellowing walls and a metal-legged table instead of a podium. On the left side of the room are my supporters—my sister, Troy, and a small contingent of former students who have come to give hugs and kind words—and a few spectators. At home more people are tensely waiting—my family and friends, and Troy's mother and brother, all of whom we have asked not to come to this humiliating public spectacle, which will include a detailed legal description of our relationship. I do not want them to see this; I am ashamed to have brought all of this upon them.

On the right side of the room, where the victim's supporters would normally sit, are row upon row of reporters, crammed together, all busily scribbling in their notepads. Them against us.

"All rise. Court is now in session. The honorable Judge Giroday presiding." The judge, a white- and blonde-haired grandmotherly woman, enters. She looks annoyed by this proceeding. I am called to the front. She speaks for a long time, ending with, "How do you wish to be tried?"

My lawyer has not prepared me for this question. He whispers sharply, "Trial by judge."

I do not miss a beat. "Trial by judge," I say softly, acting without rehearsal this scene that is my life.

"How do you plead in this matter?" she asks sternly.

"Guilty," I whisper. By uttering this one word, I have just criminally convicted myself of sexually exploiting Troy, who was under eighteen when we began our relationship and was therefore legally unable to consent to sexual contact with me.

I want to argue. Inside, I scream that I am a good person, that Troy loves me, that I have lost my career already, that we have been through enough, that I punish myself every day. I want her to understand that I am not a criminal, that I win scholarships and get straight A's, that I don't get speeding tickets, that I can't even bring myself to litter. There is a gnawing hole in my stomach. My eyes sting with tears, but I will not cry in front of the cameras.

It is all a mistake. I am sorry; I didn't know the law or the consequences. If I had left Mark when I started to feel as if my heart was being crushed in a trash compactor, none of this would have happened. If I'd known that Troy would drop out of school ten months after our relationship started, thereby making it legal, I would have waited. If I'd realized that the Crown can lay a charge even if the "victim" denies any crime took place, or if I'd known how much I was going to hurt people, how much I would miss teaching, or what this would feel like . . .

Instead, I say nothing. The judge frowns at me but avoids my eyes. She frowns more deeply at the right side of the

courtroom and admonishes the media for their sensationalistic and extensive coverage of my case. "Because he was not
yet eighteen in January of last year, Mr. Robertson cannot be
identified in any way," she says.

Troy sits tense and still beside Lisa, who looks as if she is
going to cry. The judge's words mean that in the pictures of
us leaving the courtroom Troy's face will be blurred, and that
the papers will persistently refer to him not by name but as
my victim. A pre-sentence report is ordered to determine my
level of danger to society. The lawyers confer about their
schedules and set the next court date, when my sentence will
be determined. No one asks about my schedule. Court is
adjourned for one month. I am dismissed.

Back in the passenger seat of my sister's car, I am silent.
Leaning my head against the cool glass, I can hear the reporters shouting and running after us. Listening to their
voices, holding my copy of the court conviction in my hands,
I feel nauseous. This morning, I was Heather. This afternoon,
and for every day for the rest of my life, I am a convicted sex
offender. Troy leans forward from the backseat and kisses my
head. "I love you," he says. I close my eyes, remembering.

# The Three of Us Against the World

*T*HEY ARE FIGHTING AGAIN. We are sitting at the kitchen table eating tuna fish sandwiches that my mom has made. I can almost see the words flying over my head, and I feel the hurt and anger thrown with them. My sister is too young to understand, but I know what this means.

My mom turns to me. "Is the tuna OK?" She means, does it taste funny; is it still OK to eat?

The sandwich churns in my stomach. It does taste funny. "No, it's OK," I say.

I don't know what they are fighting about, but I am sure that I do not want to make it worse. I try to sit perfectly still and eat staring at my plate. "Why do you always . . ." "It's never enough for you . . ." The phrases are familiar, lurking behind any event, any meal, any trip to the park. I wish they would get a divorce.

Suddenly I am sick; my stomach can't take the fighting or the bad tuna. I throw up at the table. I feel ashamed. I am sorry. I am sorry. My mother bends over to help me and my dad goes to the sink to get a cloth to clean up my mess. "Look what you did," she says to my dad over my head.

Weeks later the school counselor comes to the door of my Grade 6 class, talking quietly with my teacher. Right away I know she is here for me. My sister, Grade 2, is already standing outside the classroom in the cool, dim hallway. I know what the counselor will say—this is familiar—but I don't know which of our many babysitters we will have to go to after school to wait for my dad to get home from work. I hope it's not Mrs. Bastet, who is strident and fat, with short, overpermed hair so thin you can see her scalp, and who serves us Kraft Dinner smothered in ketchup while she and her thirteen-year-old daughter yell at each other.

The blonde woman with too much makeup says gently, "Your mother is in the hospital." I resent her gentle delivery and nod matter-of-factly. Lisa and I have heard this news before. Tonight, my dad will pick us up from the babysitter's, and tomorrow after work he will take us to visit our mom in the hospital.

We both hate to go, but we know it is important to my mother. Once we get to the hospital I hold my arms tight against my sides and walk down the center of the beige tiled hallway in the psychiatric ward, trying not to look into the open doors of the rooms on either side of me, trying to ignore the strange shouts and moans from inside the rooms, my heart beating fast with fear. When my mom returns home, six or eight weeks later, things will be normal until it happens again.

MY MOTHER HAS had symptoms of manic depression as far
back as I can remember. At Christmastime, I coach my sister
in which or how many toys she can ask for from the *Sears
Christmas Wish Book.* We conceal hot dog and school picture
days from my parents so as not to add fuel to their barely
concealed anger and disillusionment with each other.

I feel relief when my mom finally moves out. My sister
and I work hard to convince my dad that at eight and eleven
we are old enough to look after ourselves when we come
home from school, that everything will be OK. I take my responsibility seriously and feel sure that we will succeed as a
family despite the odds against us. My dad buys the *I Never
Cooked Before Cookbook* in paperback. The time we make the
mashed potatoes into thick soup and the time we drop the
turkey on the floor on its way out of the oven become memories of the three of us becoming a family, learning together
how to survive. Lisa and I both know that we are loved.

After my mom leaves, my family functions on a tight routine. Lisa and I visit her on alternate weekends, grocery shop
on Thursday nights, and clean the house on Saturday mornings. Anything outside the routine is an obstacle, a challenge
for which we are unprepared.

Most of our energy is spent on survival. One Saturday I
hear my father in the basement, cursing at the wires at the
back of the dryer as he tries to fix it. I sit with him downstairs, passing him pliers and carefully holding the solder
while he melts the silver liquid onto the wire ends. There is
no suggestion of calling a repairman; I understand that we
can't afford it because of the divorce, although by most standards we are not poor. "Damn," he swears, red-faced and

frustrated. The dryer is still not working. I hold my breath. Silently, I pray that his efforts will pay off and that the day will end well.

It is the three of us against the world. Some Sunday mornings my dad takes us to Granville Island for hot chocolate with whipped cream and cinnamon; other weekends the three of us go sailing, which is my dad's preferred escape from his job at the TD Bank. Otherwise, we rarely leave North Vancouver. I respect my dad's willingness to raise two daughters on his own.

I get perfect marks and have a few close girlfriends, so nobody worries about me. My friend Tamara's mom gives her a tampon for me to try, my first, and Tamara brings it to school for me. She reads the instructions through the stall door of the girls' bathroom at Argyle Secondary before school starts one morning. "I think it has to go in farther before you push the cardboard part," she explains.

"OK, I think I've got it."

When I am fifteen, I slice my finger open on the metal edge of the car door, and my next-door neighbor Katherine's mom takes me to emergency. When our cat gets sick and has to be put down, Tamara's mom drives me home from the vet while I cry beside her, holding the empty cage.

Although some days I miss having a mom, I begin to feel disdain for mothers in general. Most of the time I don't need one, and I feel that accepting mothering is a sign of weakness. I know that I am smart and independent, that I will go to university and have a career before settling down and having a family. Although I know that I will never be pretty or popular, I earn respect by being smart and athletic and having pretty friends. I like high school; I'm good at it. I play on the tennis team and get A's in everything from art to chemistry.

There is no education fund for me; I am expected to work hard in school and finance university myself. I have saved over eight thousand dollars on my own since elementary school, but I will still need to get a scholarship. Three of my friends invite me to go to Hawaii with them when we graduate from Argyle. "I'll only go if I win more than ten thousand dollars," I tell them. A few weeks before graduation, the phone rings. A man's voice says, "Congratulations, Heather. You've been selected for a Gordon Shrum Scholarship, a full four years of tuition and expenses at Simon Fraser University." It takes me five minutes to realize that he is not a telephone salesman and that my education is really going to be paid for, something I have worked towards my entire life. I have won a scholarship worth seventeen thousand dollars. I call Tamara and tell her, "I can come to Hawaii with you!"

Two months later, at seventeen, I am sitting in a lecture hall at SFU surrounded by three hundred other people, many much smarter than I am. Tamara is not here; she is going through a similar experience on the other side of the city at the University of British Columbia. I feel alone and nervous most of the time and work hard to follow the professor's voice as he lectures in a distant monotone about something called an integral. I have no time to breathe; I am submerged in an intense program of math, chemistry, biology, and physics. I study hard after classes each day. I know that if I keep going, stay focused, and work hard, my life will turn out the way it is supposed to.

# 2

# *Mark*

EIGHT-THIRTY CALCULUS CLASS. Three hundred students fill the university lecture hall. At 8:40, Mark crashes in wearing a bright pink-and-green T-shirt, his long hair tied back in a ponytail. He loudly takes a seat and, his book barely open, raises his hand. "I don't get why you put the variable out in front of the equation in line three. Shouldn't you be dividing?"

The faces of the other students are blank. Nobody else gets the equation either, but we are all dutifully copying it down. Mark is the only one with the courage to question it.

A couple of weeks later, when Mark comes in late and sits in the empty seat beside me, I turn my notes so that he can catch up. "You're always late," I say.

"Yup," he says cheerfully, with that one word flouting two of my most ingrained beliefs: that you should always be on time and that you should never call attention to yourself.

Our friendship grows in the safety of calculus class. Mark tells me that he has left Debbie, the love of his life, in Manitoba to attend SFU. He rips a brightly colored poster down from the bulletin board and scrawls a note to me across it. He writes me long letters about whether laboratory mice have orgasms and why men have nipples. He asks what perfume I wear and remembers it. When my car gets stuck in the new snow at the SFU parking lot, he jumps into the back of his truck and pulls out a shovel, digs around the tires, and yells at me to get behind the wheel and rock my car back and forth. When I feel cold in my thin Vancouver jacket, Mark has an extra sweater to lend me. I spend more and more time with him, and when I shed tears over my chemistry grade, my first ever lower than an A, he looks at me with a mixture of disbelief and pity.

BEFORE UNIVERSITY, I had never heard of Amnesty International; I had never seen a subtitled film or understood what a women's studies course might entail. I didn't know that there were subjects like linguistics or kinesiology, or that entire doctoral dissertations could be written about the mating habits of a tsetse fly. At SFU, I meet people from Richmond and Coquitlam, and from Singapore, Thailand, and Tanzania. The world is suddenly opening. I begin to drink coffee and play squash with friends after class. Although I am on a full scholarship, I quickly become aware that there are people infinitely smarter than I can ever hope to be. Mark dives with enthusiasm into this new world of university and city life and, holding my hand, drags me to hear the Vancouver Symphony Orchestra (cheap tickets) and to see a laser light show at the planetarium. We drive to Steveston and watch piles of fish being unloaded from huge rusty boats. When it rains, we lie on his floor and listen to the entire three-record set of *The Hitchhiker's Guide to the Galaxy.*

ARRIVING AT MY HOUSE one sunny day in September to do homework, Mark throws his knapsack of books into the foyer and pulls me out the door still in my socks. "It's great out here! We'll do math later. Let's go drive around."

With minor misgivings, I abandon the calculus assignment due the next day and follow him outside and on to adventure. We drive to Coquitlam, which, though just a forty-minute drive across the Second Narrows Bridge, is farther from North Vancouver than I have ever been; before I attended SFU, I had to look it up on a map. With Mark, I experience new things and see other possibilities for ways to live. I feel ready for any challenge he can throw at me.

"Want to get a Slurpee?" Mark says, veering his tan Nissan pickup wildly into a parking lot. "Sure!" I exclaim. Parked at the 7-11, he passes me my drink, then dives underneath the truck and moves something around. I can hear clanking. When he suddenly reappears, wiping his hands on a cloth he appears to keep especially for this purpose, he says proudly, "I bought this brand new when I was sixteen. My brother crashed it one week later." I cast my eyes over the rusty, dented pickup, which looks as if it has seen a war. Everyone else I know drives a car.

Mark has been out of high school for four years, so his algebra skills are rusty. Since I had a ninety-four percent average in Math 12, I tutor him after school at my family's dining room table. In return, he takes me for long drives in his truck and cooks me dinner. Mark knows how to grocery shop and cook, since he was kicked out of his mother's home at sixteen. I don't tell him how impressed I am, or how I feel an appealing wave of danger when he uses the word "fuck." He says I study too much, am too naïve, that I need to get out more. With his help I learn how to change the oil in my car. I even buy my first set of screwdrivers. We spend long nights together sitting cross-legged on the floor among his giant red, blue, and yellow pillows discussing relationships, love, and sex.

On a hike, Mark is the person who gives his only pair of mittens to a stranger with cold hands, although he will never get either the mittens or the favor returned. He talks about being emotionally naked with someone and describes how sex and love for him are intricately entwined. He believes in soul mates and underdogs. He believes that he can be an engineer and have long hair, that social conventions are for cowards, that what you learn is more important than how you feel, and that the future will always be better than the present. He talks in a completely unreligious way about acting "Jesus-like." I want to believe that the world can be like this. I believe in goodness; I am an altruist at heart. Soon he becomes my first lover.

THE MORNING AFTER our first night camping together, the air is dense and the ground is damp. I am thinking idly about last night, the easy, rambling conversation. I can still smell the campfire on my clothes this morning. We are folding the tent, but I am not doing it right. Without warning, there is rage in his voice. "You have to wrap the poles with the ground sheet, really tight so it fits in this stuff sack. No, no, no, you have to fold the tent in thirds, not in half. Look, there's still pine needles in the bottom of it! I've spent time figuring out the best way to do this, you know." When I complain about his anger, he says, "You are so good at learning things, I expect you to get them right all the time." With some discomfort, I accept this as a compliment.

To Mark, there is always a right way and a wrong way. Like my dad, he has high standards and judges harshly. Order and systems are vitally important to him. When service is slow at a checkout, he makes a point of saying something to the clerk about the lack of customer service. In his eagerness to change the world, he brushes feelings, both his and others', aside. My friends are mistrustful of his influence over me, and often find themselves engaged in tense philosophical arguments with him in social situations.

Mark is also practical. He knows how to do all the things that seemed to blindside my family—maintaining the car, cleaning the fridge, fixing the thermostat. I feel an overwhelming sense of relief that I no longer have to carry quite as much weight in the day-to-day survival of my family. I begin to lose my impression of my dad as an underdog hero struggling to raise two daughters and see through Mark's eyes that many habits I thought were absolute are not. Mark questions why we only grocery shop on Thursdays, although the fridge is empty by Tuesday. He points out how the unspoken rules that helped us as a younger family, like being home for dinner every night or spending alternate weekends at my mother's, are now often ineffective. Yet we continue to follow them, as if the structure itself will sustain us.

Being with Mark is reliable, safe. He helps my dad fix the dryer; he chops firewood for our fireplace. He likes to help. Now, three months after we had our first calculus class together, he is at my house most days. Once when Mark and I go to Whistler and I return home late for family dinner, my dad is withdrawn and short with me. "What's wrong?" I ask. "Nothing," he says, and will say nothing more. But I can sense his resentment, his feeling of abandonment, his fear of losing me to adulthood and to Mark. Although I am hurt by my dad's response, I feel sorry for him for the first time. My respect for Mark grows and becomes something like a need.

When school breaks for Christmas, Mark and I drive twenty-eight hours straight to Winnipeg to meet his family, and then ten more hours north to the frozen mining town of Thompson, where he was born. I buy winter boots and a coat especially for our trip. The temperature in Thompson is minus fifty-two degrees Celsius with the wind chill. My nose bleeds constantly from moving between the cold dry air outside and the warm dryness inside. Mark's family is friendly and warm, but Mark criticizes everything I do, from how I drag the fork on my teeth when I eat to how I wipe the toast crumbs from the counter.

At a New Year's Eve basement party, I meet Jill, who wears heavy black eyeliner and is already married at nineteen, and Carrie, pregnant with her second child at twenty-one. We struggle to find conversation about clothes and nail polish. That week, Mark arranges for me to meet his ex-girlfriend, Debbie, whom he idolizes, and we all spend a tensely silent evening at the local Ukrainian restaurant. Throughout dinner

Debbie stares at Mark, and I escape to the washroom as often as I can. Outside the snow is crisp and beautiful, but I feel as if I am packed alive in Styrofoam.

Driving back from the shopping mall two weeks into our trip, I can't take being inside any longer. "Mark, I'm going to walk the rest of the way back from the mall. I need to clear my head," I say, "and I'm desperate for some exercise." He glares at me.

"What's wrong?" I ask.

He pulls me roughly out of the truck and yanks the mitts from my hands, watching me silently. I stand still, not sure why we are doing this. Watery sun filters through the tiny ice crystals in the air around us, which in a warmer climate would be snowflakes. In less than a minute, my bare hands turn bright red and start to hurt. I reach to pull my mitts back on, but he stops me. The pain in my hands is insistent. Tears well in my eyes.

"You see?" Mark says. I nod silently, tears streaking my face. "You can't walk home from the mall. You could die out here," he says.

I understand from this that he cares about me and that this lesson is for my own good.

WHEN WE RETURN from Manitoba, Mark tells me that he has decided to leave SFU after next semester and complete his degree at the University of Alberta, which offers power engineering. We have been together over a year now. We agree that I will arrange a co-op work placement for the fall in Calgary, only three hours away from U. of A.

Camping the week before we are due to leave, I ask him

where he is staying in Edmonton while he finds a place to live. There is a pause. "With Debbie," he says carefully.

"What?" I feel ill.

"She moved to Edmonton last month. Her brothers live near there."

I have already arranged my work term in Calgary; it is too late to change it. I don't know what to say; we have not broken up, or have we? I feel the bottom dropping out beneath me.

When I move to Calgary it is my first time living away from home, and I am lonely. After work, I kneel on the floor of my mostly empty apartment and spill tears through the phone to my dad. The pain is unbearable. I still love Mark; the previous two years with him have been the most important part of my life. Mark says we are friends, he still calls me, and we meet in Banff for leaf-strewn hikes together. But I want us to be more than friends. I don't understand why he wants to be with Debbie or what I have done wrong. When my work term is over I come home with relief to the familiar warmth of Vancouver, my dad, my sister, my friends. Mark stays in Edmonton with Debbie, although I know from his letters and phone calls that they are not getting along.

One day a courier truck pulls up to my house. I feel a surge of excitement as the driver walks to my door with an envelope. The excitement vanishes when I read all thirty-two pages of the letter from Mark. Debbie has accepted an offer of marriage from someone else, someone who is not poor and struggling in university, someone with whom she can start having children immediately. Mark is angry with me; I am manipulative, a bitch. I did not stay out of their way. He never wants to see or speak to me again. My heart pounding,

I grab the box full of letters, ticket stubs, and other mementos of our relationship from the top shelf of my closet. I dump everything into the kitchen sink along with the letter and set the pile on fire. I stare at the flames. When the smoke alarm starts to wail I rouse myself and douse the flames with cold water from the tap. I am shaking.

Mark does not contact me again. More than a year later, we run into each other at the wedding of a mutual friend. I have dated only casually since his letter; my feelings for Mark are still strong. When we start to talk, the chemistry that drew us together is still there. He arranges an engineering practicum in B.C. He still corresponds with Debbie, but she is married now, safe. I do not talk about how much he hurt me, and he does not talk about how hurt he is that Debbie has married someone else. We know that we can succeed together in life, and being together makes sense. We both enjoy mountain biking and camping, do not want to have kids right away, and are eager to establish our careers. I feel happy to have him back in my life, yet I can't get over the feeling that he has settled for me. This feeling gets buried as our friends from university welcome him back into our group and Mark lands a spot in the engineer-in-training program at BC Hydro.

I GRADUATE FROM SFU's business program and then begin work on my teaching degree at UBC. Mark and I move in together in a small apartment on the sixteenth floor of a downtown building. He is cautious about marriage but agrees that living together will be a test of our relationship.

From the beginning, Mark is grumpy and on edge. He does not like the crush of people downtown, the lack of parking, the incessant sirens and traffic noise. He resents the rainy weather and constantly sneezes and itches from the B.C. trees. Because Vancouver is my home, I feel responsible for his un-happiness—for the weather, the traffic, the high cost of rental accommodation and concert tickets. When he complains my stomach churns, but I try my best to lighten his dark moods.

By contrast, I am happy. I love riding my bicycle out to my education courses at UBC and stopping for a coffee at Star-bucks on Davie Street on my ride home. I love the bicycle culture of Vancouver, the ethnic mix of people and foods, the flamboyant gay society of the West End. When I graduate with the highest marks in my university class of 250 and land an unheard-of full-time job teaching business and math at John Oliver Secondary, my world seems almost perfect. I can see success, like the flag on a golf hole, waving. I am twenty-five years old.

# 3

# Small Town

AS MUCH AS I LOVE my job, with both our incomes we cannot afford to buy even a small house in Vancouver. After two years of living in the West End, we move to the small mill town of Gibsons on the Sunshine Coast, where we can afford to buy a house, and where the beaches are beautiful and the parking spaces plentiful. Surely this choice will make Mark happier and improve our life together. I don't think about how much I will miss my friends and family or the repertory cinemas or the fragrant samosas served on Wednesdays at John Oliver. The chance to own a house and the release from city stress outweigh the fact that I have to give up a job I love and am now unemployed.

WE EMBARK ON an extensive renovation of our new home. In the evenings we take purposeful walks through the neighborhood, talking about our RRSPs and student loan payments, and whether adding more insulation will reduce our electric heating bill. When he is not talking about his work, Mark follows the electrical diagram of our house in his head, trying to sort the maze of wires into order. I have a vague sense that something precious in our relationship has been lost, but as I felt with my family, we are on a schedule, too busy to give our situation much thought. Mark does not ask me to marry him, and I do not pursue it. I try to avoid the thought that this is because he is still in love with Debbie. Once we have established ourselves, I believe, we can think about our relationship.

Gibsons is beautiful, but grocery stores close at six o'clock and video stores at ten. There are no funky coffee shops, no ethnic restaurants, and the people, overwhelmingly Caucasian, are distantly friendly but display a small-town mistrust of newcomers that is new to me. Most of the women my age are absorbed in their children, driving them to softball camp and swimming lessons. I feel isolated and overwhelmed by the amount of work that renovating a house involves. Gibsons is a forty-minute ferry ride from Vancouver, and I see my friends from there less and less. Still, I am grateful to have a house, and Mark and I have a project that will establish our lives together.

After a summer of job hunting, I land an interview at Chatelech Secondary in the nearby town of Sechelt and am offered a job. I am ecstatic and rush home to tell Mark. "In a few weeks I will have money again. I'll get to meet new people; I'll become part of the community!"

"I can't believe you got a job already! Didn't you hear that it was next to impossible to find a teaching job over here?"

"Yes, yes," I say, "but I guess they need people who can teach math. Anyway, I don't care how it happened, it happened!"

We hug roughly. It's been a long time since we've been physically affectionate. I feel a surge of warmth for Mark. We are partners in this adventure, true pioneers. It's tough, but things are going to be OK. He pecks my cheek paternally. "When I told you to have it all taken care of by Friday, I was only joking, you know."

"I know—but you know me and deadlines . . ."

Smiling, for once we are smiling. It feels good. Mark goes to the fridge to open a bottle of wine. "We'll toast to your new job," he says.

Not five minutes after the wine is poured, the phone rings. Since few people know our new phone number I feel a momentary twinge of dread. Mark answers, and his face turns serious. He hands the phone to me. A crisp voice says, "This is the Women's Medical Clinic at Vancouver General Hospital. Is this Heather Ingram?"

"Yes," I say.

"Your Pap test has indicated severe cervical dysplasia, which likely indicates cancer. I need to schedule you for a biopsy. I must warn you that you will likely need surgery fairly soon."

I can only nod. Mark's eyes follow mine. The woman on the phone is still talking, about schedules and procedures and tests. I will have laser surgery for cervical cancer in September.

LIKE CLOCKWORK, Chad and Neil, two of my Grade 10 students, greet me in the school office at 7:30 A.M. They want to use my room to launch a game of Dungeons & Dragons before

class. Chatelech's principal, Bruce Jansen, smiles at me from
his desk as I grab the pile of assignments, memos, and notes
from my box, balancing them on the pile of books in my
arms. I give some of my books to Chad and motion to Neil to
get the door. They follow me back to my room, tripping over
each other to open the classroom door.

In contrast to John Oliver, which has over 2,500 students,
Chatelech has only about 750 students, and teachers are seen
not only as authority figures but also as people, parents, and
community members. The atmosphere is less formal and is
taking me some getting used to. Every teacher at this wonderful school has an informal specialty. For Graham, it is the
top five percent of the math students, whom he inspires and
motivates to push their skills to the limit. For Christine, it is
those who need discipline and a regular, structured environment. Kel specializes in understanding social problems; he's
an expert at dealing with Jill, whose ex-boyfriend is stalking
her, and Jason and his drug problem, and Roscoe, who has
just been kicked out of his parents' house. My specialty is
evolving into the transition cases, kids who carry only one or
two alternate classes—designed for kids with behavioral
problems—mixed with regular classes. My experience in
avoiding conflict with my parents and Mark turns out to be a
useful skill in working with challenging kids.

Although John Oliver was a tough school with many
gang-related problems, having grown up in the Vancouver
area I felt more at home with the mix of kids there, predominantly Asian or East Indian, than I do with the mainly white
kids here, who are influenced by a combination of redneck
and hippy attitudes. Some of my students at Chatelech frus-

trate me, like Joel, who wanders out the door two or three times during class despite my protestations. Others, like Wendy, struggling to finish Grade 11 before her baby is due, stir my curiosity. How can I reach them? What will work? I am fascinated by this job and its complexity, and with how the culture of the Sunshine Coast adds its own twist to the challenge of teaching. The students, who have all known each other since kindergarten, display an indifference to authority for which I alternately feel exasperation and respect.

At 9:10 A.M., an announcement floats from the loudspeaker. "Students will now proceed to the gym for this morning's assembly." A cheer rises. This class is Alternate Math 10, the group I have the most trouble controlling. The kids rush out towards the gym. Jane, the social studies teacher, smiles at me. As my class mixes with the crush of other students, I realize some of my alternate kids are missing. "Jane, can you watch my kids for a sec?"

I stroll out to the parking lot, where the regulars—the smokers and skippers and those who want to be cool—are talking with their friends under a cloud of smoke. One boy revs the engine of a 1976 Mustang and turns up the thumping bass until the speakers in the car distort. Keith is standing out of sight just inside the trees, and a few more of my Math 10As are with him. I walk towards them. "All right, you guys are supposed to be in the assembly."

"Oh, Ms. Ingram, what's the point? It's a waste of time," Keith says.

"Back," I command sternly, pointing to the gym. "You go to the assembly, or I'll make you do math."

"OK, we'll go do math," Keith says innocently.

I hesitate. They are supposed to be in the assembly, but the opportunity to have six kids who desperately need the extra help captive and motivated is irresistible. Like many teachers, I feel impatient that so much class time is lost to activities like assemblies and field trips. And I'll be able to get some marking done while I'm in the classroom. "Hmmn. Well, OK, but if I don't see some serious work, you're back in the assembly."

Figuring that they have won, they are eager. "Don't worry! We'll work." Keith flashes me a victorious smile.

Since they are the only ones in the room, they get right to work. After about ten minutes of quiet, Keith says, "What's the answer to number six?" He looks at me, eyebrows raised, from his desk.

"It's seventeen, you asshole. Don't you know anything?" Erin's voice calls from behind him.

I am about to reprimand her when Keith pipes up, his voice full of delight, "Hey, I got that one right!"

I walk to his desk and see that he has written not only the correct answer but all the steps I have shown over and over again on the board. He grins at me and I smile back. It is a privilege to teach these kids, and a special privilege to have only six at a time. They are usually afraid to voice their ignorance and risk looking stupid, and so this success is rare and precious. Keith gets three pages done. Erin does four. It is my most rewarding teaching moment to date.

Later that day, Bruce Jansen stops by my classroom after school. He is a youthful and energetic grandfather with dark hair and a limp, the result of a deteriorating hip joint; he listens to teachers and students alike, gives praise generously, and even coaches one of Chatelech's volleyball teams. I am wiping the blackboard absently, thinking about the usual list of things I need to do before classes the next day. It is rare to see Bruce at my door, and I briefly wonder if I have done something wrong. "Heather, I just wanted to let you know that I think you're doing a great job. I've had some positive comments from both parents and students about you, and I thought you needed to hear about it."

I flush and smile, feeling competent, successful. "Thank you, thank you so much."

"You're welcome," he says cheerfully, and lays his hand on the door frame for support before turning back to the office.

OUTSIDE VANCOUVER GENERAL HOSPITAL, the traffic rushing by hurts my ears. Mark's face is lined and cross. We are shouting at each other above the street noise. Gray concrete surrounds us. Hot, bitter tears drop from my cheeks. Finding a parking spot started our fight—but then everything seems to be difficult with Mark. I feel as if we are always rushing, always stressed, even when we are supposed to be having fun. When I am not around Mark, his voice is still in my head, directing, criticizing. Nothing I do is right. Since we moved to Gibsons, I've been spending more and more time in my head, which is becoming my only place of refuge. I am shutting myself off from Mark, but I can't seem to fight back; I don't want to fight back. Other couples don't have these problems.

"I just want your support," I say.

"I don't know what that means," Mark yells. "I don't know how to support you!"

I fight through my tears to speak. "Look, just hold my hand. Tell me everything's going to be OK."

"But I don't know that it will. Do you want me to lie to you?" he says. I feel my stomach clench again.

If I were smarter, more aware, I would be able to see through our fight. I would understand why we are spending the ten minutes before my surgery in precisely this way and why so much of our time is spent damaging each other. My sense of despair is overwhelming. I feel that I will never be good enough for Mark, that he somehow expects me to be extra smart, loving, and competent to compensate for his loss of Debbie. Some nights we fall asleep exhausted from our emotional exchanges, which start without warning and spiral downward quickly.

"Stop hurting me," I plead.

"I'm not trying to hurt you!" he says.

I am ashamed that I cannot live up to his absolutes of right and wrong, which sound increasingly critical and range from how I drive (badly) and how I cook (not enough vegetables) to how much money I could save if I didn't stop for coffee on the way to work (three dollars a day) or how much better for the environment it would be if I biked to work instead of driving. I want to succeed, but the bar keeps moving. As I did when my parents fought, I try not to do anything wrong, have needs, or make matters worse by taking up space. I feel competent at work, but around Mark I still feel like a child. I realize that I see him more as a critical parent than as a supportive boyfriend.

Somehow we get inside the building. Tying the sterile blue gown around my neck, I shut Mark out of my heart. While the long needle of anesthetic pierces my cervix, I concentrate on the postcard of Hawaii taped to the ceiling. Mark holds my hand and finally whispers, "You're going to be OK." I close my eyes, grateful, but at the same time harder inside.

# 4

# Troy

*T*HE HALLWAY IS CRAMMED. It is class change time. As usual, my arms are crowded with books as I weave my way down the hall towards the office. If I am lucky, I can make it there, pick up my attendance sheets, and be back before the bell rings and thirty Grade 9s swarm the room. Math next. Factoring polynomials. Do I have enough handouts? Will Jesse forget his calculator again? Somewhere I have an extra one.

"HI, HEATHER." It is Ellory, the art teacher, pretty and pregnant. She looks tired. Marks are due this week. "Can you help me with my marks disk after school?" she asks.

"Sure," I call, over my shoulder.

"Hi, Ms. Ingram!" A group of girls on my right.

"Hi, you guys. Crystal, I like your new haircut." Cailen, Celeste, Matt, Trevor, Tara, Christine. Eye contact, smile.

"Hey, Jill, you owe me page ninety-three!" I say.

"By 3:30, I promise," Jill's reply floats above the din.

Familiar faces, each student unique. Be relentlessly positive, remember past conversations, ask about families, gently tease about new girlfriends or boyfriends, notice new shoes or hats, throw in advice when it's needed, listen, encourage them to try, celebrate their successes. Crazy job. I love it.

Hey, a new boy. Holy shit, what beautiful eyes. I turn back for a second look. Walking with a thin binder tucked under one arm, he is tall, just over six feet, and wearing a casual long-sleeved navy sweater with a khaki stripe across the chest and baggy jeans. Probably a skater. Short, finger-combed hair, eyes the color of a glacial lake after the sun has gone down. I feel a rush of adrenaline. He does not look at me. I wonder what he's like.

Only a moment and he is gone. My hands are tingling and my heart is racing. I have to laugh at myself. He's exactly the kind of guy I would have swooned over in high school but who would never have given me a second look.

I spot the automotive teacher. "George, can I get you to look at my car this week?"

"Talk to me at lunch!"

The first bell rings. I have three minutes. Quickly, move it, Heather.

"OK, everyone, books closed." Five-minute quiz on the board. "I know, Jesse. Here, borrow this calculator. Get those pencils moving!" A day moves forward.

"YOU'VE INCLUDED your accounts payable in your assets—that's why you're not balancing."

Tara looks at me and frowns, "What's accounts payable again?"

"Money that you owe, usually to a supplier," I say.

"Oh yeah—so it's a liability!" she says.

"Ah-ha!" I reply. "Such brilliance."

Tara smiles and starts erasing, eager to see the numbers balance, eager to feel the joy of a problem solved, the excitement of understanding what she's doing. Success is a rare feeling for some of these kids. My accounting class is full of the ones who may not make it, those who have struggled and given up, those for whom graduation is an almost unreachable goal. This is my daily challenge: to break the material down into pieces they can handle, to provide context and relevance for whatever subject we are studying, to celebrate a small triumph.

A week after he walked by me in the hallway, Troy, the new student, is in my Accounting 11 class. From across the room, I spy Greg chatting with him and say loudly, "Greg, do you need a hand?" The class turns to Greg, who quickly lowers his head and moves his pencil innocently. I make my way over to that side of the room, circulating, keeping my eyes open for puzzled expressions.

"Want some help?" I ask Troy. He is wearing a black V-necked jersey and loose-fitting black pants, belted low on his hips. His sandy brown hair looks as if it will go instantly blond in the summer. With his good looks and long, slim body, he could be a Calvin Klein model. But he sits with the underachievers in the class and appears to have little academic ambition. I am attracted to him in a detached way, as if I am watching James Dean in a movie. I remember my sponsor teacher during my teaching practicum telling me that he didn't fall in love with students much anymore. I was shocked at the time, but at this moment I can understand how easy it would be.

Since I spoke, Troy's eyes have been following me intently, and when I get closer to his desk he shakes his head once, to indicate he's fine, no help required. He rarely speaks in class; some kids are like that. I glance at his page and see that he's made an adding error. I also notice that his progress through the accounting book is slower than it should be. Automatically I wonder if he is registered in the alternate classes for his other subjects, whether he has a learning disability, or whether his reluctance to work is a result of sitting next to Greg. I make a note to keep tabs on him in class. "Better check those totals," I say, moving past his desk.

He growls at me in response, trilling his tongue against the roof of his mouth. It is an overtly sexual sound and the students around who hear him look up in surprise. They laugh and watch me to see how I will handle the situation. By his casual posture, his chair pushed far away from his desk, and his black clothes, I guess that Troy is a tough guy, admired by other students for his audacity and attitude. His extended eye contact with me seems intended to establish that he is different, in control of the situation. I look at him directly, taking in his long eyelashes, the black jacket casually thrown on the desk in front of him, the cigarette-pack bulge in his shirt pocket. He is stunningly beautiful in an almost feminine way, but there is also vulnerability combined with cocky self-confidence. It reminds me of Mark in our calculus class years ago. He looks at me with an air of conspiratorial good humor. He seems to be saying, "You and I both know that this teacher-student thing is all a big game."

It is not unusual for a male student to use his sexuality in such an overt way. The examples occur daily. "She's hot, what a babe," is overheard in smoke pit discussions about Nicolle, Chatelech's youngest female teacher. Jared, a good-looking Grade 12 student, gallantly asks Nicolle to dance, and she turns him down with a flattered smile in front of the other teachers. At John Oliver, a Grade 12 student invited one of my colleagues out for coffee after school. A group of boys in a Grade 11 art class speculates about which female teachers wear thong underwear. Many young female teachers have male students with crushes on them; it is relatively common to overhear conversations about which student would like to have sex with which teacher. I am flattered to have garnered such attention.

There are no alarm bells going off in my head, and I treat the incident with Troy as if it is no big deal. If it will establish an IOU system—I'll let you get away with this if you'll be well behaved and do your work without hassle—then I will have won something. Troy is testing me, that much is clear, but he does not seem to intend disrespect. Instead, his eyes speak a small request: "Please don't cut me down too harshly, not in front of my friends."

I hold his eyes for a minute, communicating that in choosing my response I am saving his reputation but that it will only happen once. Rolling my eyes to the ceiling, I give an exaggerated sigh. "Thanks for the *compliment,* but those totals aren't going to balance themselves." One corner of Troy's mouth lifts upward before he bends his head to work. We have both won this round.

As the school year moves on, Troy persists in his growling noises, though more subtly since that first time, and in staring

at me both in class and in the hallway. He begins to come to
class five minutes early, chats with me about the new brakes for
his Hyundai, and even asks for some help with his assignments.
For now, I do not take his attention seriously but grow accus-
tomed to it as his way of communicating. There is a marked
improvement in his attendance and in the amount of work he
accomplishes during class. But over the next few months, Troy
starts to push the boundaries of student-teacher protocol. He
stands a foot closer to me than is appropriate and compliments
me on my clothes. When I tell him to get to work, he looks at
me lingeringly, expectantly, almost as if he knows me. Or he
whistles, and I turn my head to see him gazing at me, head
tilted to the side, appreciating me.

Now when Troy walks by me in the hallway, he makes direct eye contact for as long as I will let him; he turns his body
towards me as I walk down the hall, his palms open in front of
him. He seems almost to enjoy my reprimands, mocking me
with a smile that makes me smile too. If the hallway is
crowded or I am standing talking to another teacher, he
catches my eye and nods at me, or walks by and brushes my
arm deliberately. I feel special, selected, happy.

On the field during a fire drill, he offers his umbrella in a
flourish of mock chivalry. He drops by my classroom every
morning, asks how I am, and listens intently to my response
while I go about preparing for class. I know it is inappropriate,
yet his manner is so light and casual that I do not discourage
it. It feels harmless to enjoy these attentions; I feel I deserve
this tiny break of flattery in my day. As long as our contact
does not progress beyond mild flirtation, I tell myself, I am
not hurting anybody by allowing it to continue. At the same
time, I am mildly ashamed of my own weakness and vanity.

I do not get this kind of attention at home. It has been a long time since Mark looked at me with desire in his eyes or without a cordless drill in his hand and a drywalling instruction on his tongue. We haven't been intimate for weeks, and more and more I don't even want to let him get close to me. It feels safer, less emotionally harmful, to close myself off to Mark the way I did during my surgery, to deal with him at the level of bank statements and car maintenance.

TWO MONTHS LATER, on a warm April day, Christine, one of my Grade 10s, says, "Troy has a crush on you, Ms. Ingram. He said that when he graduates, he's going to ask you out."

"I'm sure he's not serious," I say.

She shakes her head vigorously in disagreement, "Uh-huh."

I think ahead a year and wonder what I would say to decline such an offer, since it is not even a possibility. My life with Mark is an absolute, a fact of existence.

The other students seem to accept Troy's interest in me, and the fact that I dismiss these tales when I hear them seems enough to dispel any alarm among students or staff. I feel mildly guilty for enjoying Troy's attention, but my heart lifts a little each day when he walks by.

{ 5 }

# Loneliness

Y SURGERY HAS cleaned out the offending cells, and aside from checkups every three months, I can put the experience behind me. My body no longer feels quite so much like a traitor. Slowly, Mark and I toil to give our boxy 1970s house some character by painting, drywalling, and laying tile. When we are working together at something, our relationship gets easier. Choosing flooring or installing plumbing for a new sink in the bathroom, we smile and feel proud of our efforts. Mark says, "If we can survive drywalling a vaulted ceiling together, then we can survive anything!" A couple for almost ten years now, we are a part of each other's identity.

It is June, just before classes break for the summer, and though we have only been in the house for a year, Mark comes home one day to tell me that BC Hydro wants him to go up to Hudson's Hope. We get out the map. Hudson's Hope is a fourteen-hour drive north, but this is nothing new; Mark has gone on business trips before.

"How long?" I ask absently.

"Six months," he says.

Wow. Six months. How will I manage? There are holes in the wall; the baseboard heaters are disconnected and lined up to be painted in the basement. We have a huge yard with encroaching blackberry bushes.

"It's an incredible opportunity for me to learn more as an engineer. If I do well enough, I can start consulting, make more money, work from home more." He looks excited and nervous about the prospect.

I nod. "We'll be OK. It's important for your career."

We barely think twice about accepting this situation. Somehow we will make it work. Many of our couple-friends are working and living in different places from each other. Most of the women have professional jobs, which they cannot just leave to follow their husbands when companies send them somewhere else. When Mark says, "All of the older engineers in my department are divorced," I think, those men were in traditional roles and traditional relationships. We are a modern couple, equal. I can handle things by myself. It cannot happen to us.

"OH FUCK." The paintbrush I am holding spirals elegantly down towards the floor, and I watch it helplessly from the top of my ladder. The freshly painted bathroom ceiling looks good, but summer sweat drips from my hairline and now there is a messy purple splotch on the new tile floor. Oh well, it's latex; at least it'll clean up well. I climb down from the ladder and sigh.

Lonely, it's so lonely here. I haven't spoken to anyone in two days. Between Mark's long hours at work and our renovation, we haven't made more than a few casual acquaintances in Gibsons. My family is always a phone call away, but some days I just crave contact with people, and even go to the hardware store just so I can chat with the woman at the till. It is only August 5, but already I can't wait to start teaching, to be busy and social again. Mark won't be back from Hudson's Hope until November. Outside, the grass grows reproachfully. Tomorrow, I promise myself, I will cut the lawn.

Finally, it is September. I have been going up to prep for my classes since the school opened August 20, and I feel organized and prepared for the intense schedule that faces me. I will be teaching seven different courses this semester, including two alternate classes and two split classes—at least I won't be bored. When the students arrive, tanned and taller than they were in June, their energy feels good. I throw myself into my teaching responsibilities with enthusiasm. Having been at Chatelech for one full year now, I have friends among the staff, and the students I have taught are full of summer stories. Even Troy is back, and when I walk by he whistles. Nobody seems to hear him, so I just smile; some things haven't changed.

One cloudy October morning, Donna Robertson, Troy's mother and a teaching assistant in the alternate program at Chatelech, comes to see me. "Troy has a schedule conflict with two of his courses," she says. We are standing at the door of my Math 9 classroom, and I am half listening to her, half watching my students—some with clear concentration on their faces, others puzzled, some passing erasers, others punching calculators. "I know it's an imposition, but could you let him finish his accounting in one of your other blocks?"

"I guess so," I say. "He can come do his work during my prep block. My room's always full of kids getting extra help anyway."

A routine begins. Troy shows up to complete his Accounting 11 during my prep in C block. For the first few weeks he is quiet, working fairly diligently, chatting with me briefly about his friends and his other classes. I am quiet too, typing up math tests or marking accounting assignments. There are other kids in the room, some my students and some not, and most of them are focused on their assignments.

By November two more kids, Troy's friends, are following him to C block. Daniel wears a red sports jersey and has a stubbly shaved head. Jeff is smaller, skinny and edgy looking. I'm afraid they will disrupt the quiet atmosphere, so one day I tell them, "You can stay, but you have to do something productive." Hauling out the beginning accounting text and workbook, I put them to work. "Deal?" I ask.

"Hey, Ms. Ingram," Daniel says, "if we finish this stuff, do we get credit for the course?"

"If you do the assignments, and write and pass the tests, you'll get credit, same as anyone else."

"Cool," says Daniel.

I now have a mini-class of three students. It is casual, enjoyable, and with his friends there, Troy begins to talk more—about hockey, movies, who's been suspended, who's pregnant, who's in trouble with the police. I gradually get to know and care about these boys, their families, and their history in school.

"I don't mind," I say, in response to Mark's questions over the phone about teaching during my prep block. "You should meet them. They remind me of you when we first met."

"What do you mean?" Mark says.

"Well, they've never even been to a real coffee shop, they've never had a latte. You know what I'm saying?"

I feel that Mark is checking up on me with these phone calls, making sure I'm doing things in the house and carrying on our life in the right way. "Don't let it take up too much of your time. They're just a bunch of hard cases," he says.

I hear negativity, judgment, and I try to explain. "They're so worldly about some things, like swearing and smoking, and yet so completely ignorant of the good things in the world. I mean, it's really amazing. The school liaison police officer was in my class, and they all just about bolted when they saw her. I want them to believe in themselves more, not be so afraid. Everyone thinks they're real badass kids, but they have so many good qualities too."

"So you're trying to save them?" Mark asks.

"Maybe," I say. "Maybe I think I can show them that they can succeed at something, or maybe I just want them to know that they can be part of the society that they think has rejected them. They're underdogs, you know? Just like you were once."

"Hmm. Well, just be careful. You don't want to leave anything lying around; they might steal it."

Mark is so far from the person he was at university. I wonder, would we even fall in love if I met him today?

ON THE PHONE from Hudson's Hope Mark sounds happy, exhilarated, working twelve or fourteen hours a day, solving electrical problems, and learning how to rewind a generator. He is a born engineer, and I envy his passion and confidence. Long distance, he explains how to reconnect the baseboard heater I have been struggling with each day after work for a week. "You just find the power wire and connect that, then . . ."

Feeling hopelessly incompetent, I interrupt, "There are three wires. How do I know which one is power?"

"Well, it depends on the color. One of them's neutral. Black is ground. You should know this; you got an A in physics."

He sounds impatient, frustrated with me. In old jeans and a paint-covered T-shirt, I lean against the wall with a familiar sinking feeling.

Mark's impatient sigh washes over me. I feel so incompetent, so childlike when I talk to him. At work I manage 150 students a day, professional committees, staff meetings, parent-teacher meetings. At home, I can't even handle a simple baseboard heater. I am starting to hate this house with its endless stream of jobs that need to be done. I am starting to hate my own inability to cope. Mark sounds so happy in Hudson's Hope. Get a grip, Heather, I tell myself. Take a deep breath. I breathe in, but something catches in my throat, and a weak, desperate sound emerges.

Without warning, there are tears rolling down my cheeks. I don't even know why I am crying. I try to listen, try desperately to understand Mark's emphatically spaced instructions. I scribble some notes. Through the phone lines, Mark senses my distress. "It's not that hard," he says, trying to be encouraging. "I know you can do it."

"I know I can too," I say, "It's just . . ." I can't finish the sentence. "It's . . . nothing. I'm just lonely, I guess." I am hungry for someone to understand me, to feel with me, to cry or laugh with me.

"I'll be home soon," he says, unable to conceal his contentment. He loves his work, loves living in the small, familiar northern town.

I don't tell him what's upsetting me. It will do no good to tell him that he sounds happier when he is away than I ever see him at home, that this life we have created feels like a thing apart from me, or that we no longer have any fun. I feel that I am too young to feel this old, that I am drying up inside from holding everything together by myself. I know these things are my fault. When he is away, he is himself, and I am myself. I am not so stressed. I can decide with confidence what music I feel like listening to or what I want to eat for dinner. When we are together we lose ourselves.

We have fed our relationship with mortgages and RRSPs and approval from our parents. It has become so heavy that it is crushing us. We are supposed to be doing this, it is how to create a life, and all our well-educated professional friends are creating these structures too. We have been taught that jobs are scarce, that a university degree is essential, that buying a home and having other couples over for dinner is the way to achieve adult happiness. We both see this happiness as some distant future state that can be attained and then enjoyed, like a new sport utility vehicle.

Yet I no longer know who I am. In front of my class, I feel strong and competent, and I smile and make decisions and help kids learn. At home I can do nothing right, and I am not sure I can endure the time it will take to achieve our dream. I am a failure, living for a future that I don't even know if I want, and I am starting to doubt that we will ever achieve happiness. We can't give each other what we need; our only expertise lies in wounding each other.

When Mark complains about me I rarely fight back anymore. I have taken myself away. I am a machine—solid, dependable, and ugly. I work, plan the house, play tennis with women who seem normal and well-adjusted, and go through my days. Impatience surfaces in my voice suddenly and for no reason, but I ignore it.

I do not think about leaving Mark. Since our trip to Manitoba many years ago, I have been welcomed by his family as an intelligent, articulate match for their son. His dad sends me birthday cards; we ski with his brother and sister-in-law on long weekends. When his mother visits, the three of us spend hours talking, sightseeing, or planning the garden. Mark and I host Christmas at our house; he and my dad go sailing together. Our lives, our families are permanently intertwined. He knows me so well. He can pick out what I will want on a menu or my favorite passage from a book. I love him like I love my father—unconditionally—because he is familiar, because he seems to have always been there, because he is a part of who I know as me. We are like the concrete foundation of a house for each other—heavy and unmoving, but necessary. We have grown up together, and he is my identity.

If someone asked, I might be able to articulate that something essential—the thing that makes me, me—is drowning. I don't want to wait for the future to be happy. I miss the long drives of discovery we used to take; I miss going to the planetarium, drinking a Slurpee, solving world issues, and listening to each other's theories on love. The problem is, Mark won't do these things with me anymore—at least, I don't think he will. By now I am afraid to ask him. I also miss feeling that I am a young, attractive woman and that Mark wants to know me, not change me.

"You should join a club," Mark says over the phone. "Take up pottery."

EVERY OTHER DAY I teach Math 9 in room 204, across a courtyard from the alternate class. Designed to help kids who have severe behavior, drug, family, or learning problems, the class is filled with many kids from my accounting and math alternate classes. Today I am at the board, explaining to my Grade 9s how to solve simple algebraic equations. There is a figure pressed against the glass in the class across the courtyard. I recognize him, and I feel a twitch of excitement. Suddenly my hair feels shinier than it did a minute ago; my skin feels smoother.

Turning to the whiteboard, I try to ignore him. "Jessica," I say, "can you add these two terms together?" Hearing her name, Jessica whips her head around from talking to her friend in the seat behind her to face the board and smiles at me blankly. I raise my eyebrows at her and continue. Across the courtyard, he is still there, standing, watching me.

Troy raises his fingers to his lips and blows a kiss through the glass from the other room. It hits me like a real kiss. He has never been this overt, this directly sexual with me before. All of a sudden I feel scared. I have let this go too far: my job could be in danger. At the same time I feel a shot of happiness—like I imagine heroin would feel—that I know will last for the rest of the day. If I could live on this feeling instead of food, I would. I feel joyful, as if he is a regular guy who likes me, and I am a regular girl who is hoping to get asked out. But we are not regular; for the first time I think I may have to talk to Troy about his behavior. He grins and steps back from the window, mission accomplished.

Looking around the classroom, I check to see if anyone has noticed the sudden smile on my face, but everyone is oblivious to my emotions. I am safe in my teacher's role, invisible. OK, I promise myself, if I can keep this feeling, I will mark tests alone all evening; I will smile when Mark, just back from Hudson's Hope, complains that there aren't enough vegetables in the dinner I've made instead of making love to me after six months away.

After school I am in Kel's room, talking about Amanda's progress, Ryan's absences, the meeting with Kevin's dad tomorrow, and other student issues we share. Our conversation turns philosophical, and I say, "I don't know why I ended up working so well with alternate students. Maybe it's because I'm a conflict avoider."

Kel says, "Me too. But you know, Heather, I think that there's a bit of 'alternate' in you too."

# Suspended

*W*HEN TEACHERS TALK about the need for alternative education, they are talking about students like Troy. His world has rules, but they are not the same as the ones most of society, including me, lives by. Troy does not recognize formal authority except as an inconvenience or obstacle. Be loyal to your friends, mind your own business, don't mess with someone else's woman, prove your strength when you have to, and apply swift retribution to anyone who breaks the code; these are the rules by which he lives. I admire how he flouts authority and ignores social conventions that don't suit him, and I wish I could be strong and confident enough to do the same.

In his world women are either girlfriends or whores, and a man is dominant no matter what his age. I am attracted by the simplicity of it all. I'm also attracted by the sense that he views me as somehow above little-girl gossip and backbiting, as the ultimate in girlfriend material, a mature woman who does not whine or play games. I like this image of myself.

Stunningly beautiful, and completely unconscious of it, Troy has a constant stream of young girls following him around, saying his name slowly, savoring it. He drives too fast, smokes too much marijuana, and is casual with his money. I don't want to live that way myself, but I'm attracted to how completely he lives in the moment.

One day Troy and his friends come into the room and take their seats. There is an unusual energy around Troy, and I am curious but do not say anything. When Jeff and Daniel have started their chapter tests, he looks at me and says, "My dad called last night." I know from talking to his mother that she has been divorced for a long time and that Troy's dad left their family without support when Troy was very young.

"When was the last time you talked to him?" I ask.

"I've never even known him," he says. "My dad left when I was six months old."

I can't decide if I am more shocked by his dad's sudden phone call or by the fact that Troy is telling me about it. He seems to be searching for something in my eyes. "Are your parents divorced?" he asks me.

I nod. "My mom left when I was eleven."

"Then you know what it's like."

I pause, and look around the room. Jeff and Daniel are bent over their tests, pretending intently not to listen.

"Your situation is different," I say. "I still was able to see my mom. You never even got to know your dad."

"Yeah," he says. "I'm pretty pissed off at him." We are both silent for a moment. Daniel and Jeff are now openly watching our exchange. Troy shrugs his shoulders casually. "Whatever. It doesn't matter." He seems annoyed with himself.

At the end of the block, the bell rings and the boys stand to leave.

"Hey, Troy," I say to him as he gathers his books, "you have a right to be pissed off." His eyes hold mine as I silently count to five. Then he lifts his chin and turns to leave.

On the way out the door, Daniel hangs back. "I've known Troy for five years, and that's the deepest conversation I've ever heard him have with anyone."

I THOUGHT I WOULD BE happy to have Mark home from Hudson's Hope, but his rules and lists seem foreign to me. Forced to deal with the house and the community by myself, I have adapted. "You seem more independent," Mark says, surprised. I play tennis in the local women's league and I have accomplished hard-won changes in the house, which more and more feels like mine alone. When Mark complains about the smell of my coffee or the crumbs I have left on the kitchen counter, I barely listen. My heart is colder. I am surviving, even thriving in this small town.

One night soon after Mark returns, we host a dinner party. The house is not as I would like it; there are still holes in the drywall where Mark has been rewiring steadily since he got back, and the plywood floor glares at me reproachfully. But the walls are freshly painted, three subtle shades of grayish-green over which I agonized, and Mark has made fresh mushroom soup, which smells wonderful and looks elegant in the white china my mother gave us when we bought the house. Even if the table is only painted particleboard, it is clean of drywall dust. I have spent the day vacuuming and wiping down every surface. Mark has chopped and stirred all day. Everything is prepared. We are tired already.

Daren and Elaine sit across the table. Wearing a navy V-necked sweater and beige chinos, Daren is clean-cut, tall and slim. Like Mark, he is an engineer at BC Hydro. Elaine, his Asian girlfriend, is wearing size three Gap jeans and black boots from her extensive footwear collection, and has just passed her chartered accountant exam. She holds a glass of wine between her index and middle fingers, exuding energy. Daren sits on the edge of his seat as he and Mark talk about Hydro.

"If the old guys would just listen to us things would change, but they're stuck in the dark ages of engineering. They still think like a monopoly, not a customer-service-based company," Mark says to Daren. They are deep in conversation, enjoying themselves.

"How's your pottery class, Elaine?" I ask.

"It's going great, but I wish I had more time to do it. I'm at the office sixty hours a week. If I could quit my job and make a living making cups and bowls, I'd do it in a second." She sighs. I nod my agreement. I look around the table and see an undercurrent of stress on everyone's face. We are successful. We are lucky.

We finish the meal and load the dishwasher. Elaine has joined the conversation about how to solve BC Hydro's problems. My mind goes somewhere, anywhere, away from pressure, away from this structure, this conversation that feels increasingly stale and irrelevant. Tonight, after Daren and Elaine are in our spare bedroom, Mark will want me. But I don't want to have sex. Mark satisfies me in the traditional sense of that word—he is an expert at making my body feel good—but more and more I don't want him to. I don't want to let go of my body or my mind, even for an hour. I am scared that I will never get them back. I feel removed from myself, dislocated. I want to have a conversation about something besides work. I want to feel alive.

By ten o'clock we are all yawning. Tomorrow is Sunday. Daren and Elaine will be up early tomorrow to play multiple rounds of golf; they are eager to try out Daren's new clubs. Mark and I will spend the day in the attic, sweating and itching, installing another layer of fiberglass insulation. Monday morning Mark will get up at 5:15, shower, put on his white shirt and the purple tie I bought him for his birthday. At ten to six, I will drive him to the ferry for his two-hour commute into Burnaby. By 7:30, I will be at the school, hoping for fifteen minutes to get my classroom ready before the kids waiting at my door for help with their math homework or their personal life flood in. From then on, I will be running, juggling, dealing with things that need to be dealt with. At 4:00 P.M. I have a staff meeting. At 5:30 I will cook dinner before I pick Mark up at the ferry. After dinner we will finish the insulation.

"Good dinner," Mark yawns after we have finished cleaning up and gone to bed.

"Great soup," I agree.

"'Night." He rolls over.

"Goodnight." I lie awake beside him, breathing relief. We will not have sex tonight. I drift off, my body and my soul untouched. I feel myself drying up inside, cracking and checking like firewood. I must remember to call Todd's mom on Monday about his interim report. Maybe tomorrow I will get to finish marking my Grade 10s' tests.

EVERY DAY I DRIVE MARK to the ferry before the sun is up. After that, the day is mine. I dress and grab a cup of coffee at the Daily Roast on the way to work. The charm of a smaller school: my students know how I take my coffee, and they can tell what kind of day I'm having. They comment on my hair or my new shoes and wave enthusiastically when I see them on the street. Parents of kids I teach greet me in the grocery store, ask about my house renovation, and talk about their kids' grades when I take my car in to be serviced. Although I am unnerved by how "public" teaching in a small town is, I am starting to feel like a part of this community.

Each morning my room fills with kids, some with coffee, some alert and early, some bleary-eyed and late, all here for their first block Accounting 11/12, a split class. The class is self-paced, making it a natural fit for the kids who need it as their math credit for graduation. I work with Kel, the alternate teacher, to set up programs for even the toughest students. Everyone has something to do, and I walk around helping students when they get stuck.

Although he is not in this class, Troy knows many of the kids in it, and like clockwork he takes a bathroom break from his morning English class and comes to visit them. I suspect that he is also here to see me, and I look forward to his smile, which makes my skin tingle. He stays a few minutes, chats with his friends, and makes eye contact with me or blows me a kiss when no one is looking.

One Tuesday morning, Tara looks up from her book halfway through the class and says, "Where's Troy?" I laugh to think that his visits have become so regular that he is missed.

"He got suspended," Greg says to Tara.

"For what?" I ask Greg.

"Smoking weed, I think." Greg is brief, cautious, not wanting to betray his friend to a teacher.

"How long?" I ask.

"Three days."

I feel a surge of disappointment and frustration. Although the school's policy about marijuana is clear, it does nothing to address the reality that many kids smoke it regularly and even do much harder drugs. Many get the stuff from their own parents. Drug use is rampant on the Sunshine Coast. A three-day suspension. I would rather have a kid stoned but in class absorbing some of the lesson than at home where he can do drugs full-time. With borderline students whose attendance is sporadic anyway, every day that you can keep them in class is important. Troy's attendance and work are steadily improving. I suspect much of that has to do with his crush on me, but still, he is coming to class and earning a solid B.

At lunch time I search out Donna in the special needs classroom, where she is helping a Grade 8 Down's syndrome kid with his social studies. Donna is about fifty and pretty, with soft brown hair and tired eyes that seem to be waiting for the next crisis she will have to handle. Her gentle nature hides steel. "Yes, he's suspended," she sighs. "I wrote him a letter this morning before work. Sometimes that's the way we communicate best."

"Maybe I can talk to him," I say.

She looks at me, hopeful. "Well, he won't listen to me anymore. You know, he says you're the best teacher he's ever had."

I wonder if I can do any good. Troy speaks so little that I am not sure whether he will take any advice from me. "Maybe

I'll take his books out to him. That way he might not get so behind, especially if you can convince him to do some over Christmas break."

I don't know if I can help, but I do know that he will do school work for me as for no other teacher. Maybe I can use this flirtation to give him something of value—or at least someone to talk to. And yet my intentions are not pure. I feel myself falling into the seductive illusion of being needed, of being important enough to make a difference in someone's life.

After school, I drive with Daniel to Troy's house. My heart is beating fast. Daniel, sitting in the passenger seat, is talking about his new girlfriend; he thinks he is falling in love with her. Listening to him talk about his feelings, I become more conscious of my own. I would not drive on my own time to take books to every student. I feel a sense of adventure and of the unknown, a hint of danger, and nervousness. I want to know if he wants me the way I am afraid I am starting to want him. If there is something between us, this encounter will demonstrate it. On his home turf, I will be able to read something in his face about whether he feels anything like I do. If the answer is no, I will turn around and go home, no harm done. But if I see yes, what then?

Daniel stops talking. Suddenly I ask, "Do you think Troy's addicted to pot?"

He shrugs. "No more than I am. No more than half the people on the Sunshine Coast." Daniel points to the wrought iron gate. We are here. The yard is big and wild with trees and flowers. The trailer is small but painstakingly painted and maintained. Three cars are parked out front, all in various stages of repair. Pulling my car into the dirt driveway, I feel out of my element. Jokes about trailer parks flip through my mind, and I realize that this is the first time I've been to a home that did not have at least two bathrooms. Suddenly I am ashamed of my protected North Vancouver upbringing; this is the home of a single mother struggling against poverty, trying to provide the best for her two nearly grown sons.

Looking perfectly at home in a plaid work jacket with a beer in his hand, Troy leans under the hood of his car. He does not appear to be shamed by his suspension; he looks as if he is beyond high school, beyond trivial rules and punishment. He looks adult.

"Hey, man," Daniel says.

"Hey," Troy replies. His eyebrows are raised but he nods at me and smiles. The three of us go inside. "Want a drink?" He opens the fridge door and pulls out a carton of store-bought eggnog.

"Thank you," I say. "I brought you your books—thought you might want to keep up with the class."

The ceiling in the trailer is low, and the fuchsia living room carpet has a sweeping, almost artistic, stain. Troy notices my stare and says, "My mom did that to camouflage the bleach that someone spilled on the floor."

The three of us sit in the kitchen, silent. I think I have made a mistake by coming; he seems embarrassed to have me here. Troy wipes at the grease smudges on his face. "I guess you know why I got suspended," he says.

"Greg told me," I say. "You know, smoking pot on school grounds is . . ." I don't know what to say to him about his suspension. "We all miss you in class," I say finally. He nods, then gets up, as if he has heard what I was going to say before.

"Do you want to meet Joey?" He walks to a large cage in the corner of the kitchen and gently pulls out a small yellow bird. Joey seems used to this and sits comfortably on his shoulder. Troy nuzzles the bird with his cheek, repeating softly, "Hi, Joey. Hi, big guy . . ." He holds the bird out to me, and I stroke its tiny head with my finger. We are silent, looking at each other, the bird between us. I am going crazy. There is no reason for me to be here, no reason I should feel anything for this young man. I am his teacher, that's all.

"I should get going," I say, breaking the spell.

"Wait," Troy says. He walks with Joey on his shoulder to a room at the other end of the trailer and then emerges with a box wrapped in Christmas paper. "Open it," he says.

I lift the tape neatly and unwrap a box of chocolates. The card says, "To Ms. Ingram, from Troy Robertson." It is so out of character for him and reminds me so much of a little kid's sweet offering that I almost cry.

"It's to thank you for being so nice to me," he says. He moves toward me, and we hug briefly.

"Thank you for the gift," I say.

Troy holds his accounting books under one arm as we walk together out to the car. As I sit down to drive home to my normal life, I think of the contrast between what he projects at school and the person I have inadvertently seen. He walks around to the passenger door, looking tall and handsome, mischief in his eyes. "I'd like to take you out sometime," he says. I laugh out loud, and feel a shot of adrenaline, sweet like candy floss, surge through my stomach.

"You have to graduate first," I say, still laughing. I'm trying to talk myself out of it, but I feel like I am falling in love. The implications are so enormous that they make my knees shake and my stomach twist with terror. I am sad too, because I know that a relationship with Troy simply cannot be. There is so much pleasure in having this beautiful young man lean his lean body over the hood of my car and ask me out. But this moment can only be a moment, and part of its charm comes from its sheer impossibility.

Troy pats his pockets for a cigarette, then changes his mind. For a minute I wonder if I've hurt him. "We need to stop," I say finally, looking up at the clear sky. "It's going to get me in trouble." He nods. We have reached an understanding.

WHEN CHRISTMAS BREAK ARRIVES, Mark and I work on the house, but my thoughts are at school. I miss Mark when he is away, but the more he goes away, the more I grow used to his absence. Now I don't really want him here. I avoid his touch, which is easy when we're tired from insulating the attic all day. I'm afraid that if we do touch I will lose control, start sobbing and maybe never stop.

I don't miss Troy over the break, but I think about him idly when I am grocery shopping or weeding the garden. He embodies living for the moment, knowing what's important in life, tenderness, caring, wholeness. He is satisfied with who he is and what he has, even though by my standards he has almost nothing. I am rarely satisfied with things. My house needs new floors; my math classes are not achieving enough; my relationship with Mark is stagnant. Through Troy's eyes I can see what it means to be happy, or at least what it means to know that happiness is within your grasp. Friends, something to do on Friday night, working transportation,

enough money for a six-pack and a submarine sandwich—
these things are enough for him. I know that they are not
enough for me, or at least that they would not be for long, but
right now they feel like an answer, or an escape.

I resolve that I will find more friends. And I will tell Mark
exactly how I feel.

## { 7 }

# Crossing the Line

*T*HEY ARE HERE. It is Friday night, January 15, 1999, and Mark is away skiing with a friend for the weekend. I knew they might come; they had joked about it in class. I know if I let them in, there will be no turning back. I know that even by watching TV with these boys, eighteen years old, I am crossing a line.

The responsible adult in me is scolding and reproachful. The girl who stayed home with her little sister, who tried so hard to be responsible, who watched her parents struggle and fail to find happiness in their lives, who worked and worked to build a life with Mark, wants to say yes. Please, just one night of fun. Just one night to be myself. Nothing will happen, I promise. I won't let anything bad happen. I step back from the open door.

I am not thinking beyond the next minute. As they walk through the door, inhabiting my space with their long legs and their energy, pressing strange rap music from my CD player, I feel salvation. My hands are shaking. They are polite but utterly self-assured. I am anything but the calm, handle-anything teacher who runs her classes efficiently and devotes long hours to marking and prep. Troy is here, in my house. I feel a wave of dread, coupled with sparks of adrenaline. I am stepping out of an airplane, hang gliding, bungee jumping—pick one. I am doing all the things I never would in real life.

This is not real life—look, I have proof, there are three eighteen-year-old boys in my house. They have come to see me, not because I am mature and responsible and a straight-A student or a good daughter, but because I am still young and fun and attractive. Of all the places they could be tonight, of all the beautiful young girls around and alcohol-drenched parties they could be attending on this Friday night, they have chosen to come to my half-renovated house, to my bor-ing, safe, dutiful life. Beyond flattered, I feel included as I never was, part of the gang. For the first time, I see only the next step in front of me. I know this is wrong, but I don't feel that I am hurting anyone. They want this, they planned this. It's as if I have been given a surprise party; I feel special for the effort that has been taken.

They have come prepared with movies, video games, and a twenty-six of Long Island iced tea stuffed into a backpack that they hide furtively, waiting for the right time to bring it forth. Troy and I lie on our stomachs in the basement of the house Mark and I share, and compete with our video race cars. "I'm horrible!" I wail.

"You're right, you suck," Troy smiles. He speeds ahead and sends his race car careening back to block my slow, wobbly car, which I am trying desperately to keep on the constantly moving track.

Daniel asks, "Can we make pizza?" The four of us ladle sauce and layer salami. Troy grates the cheese.

"No, you idiot," Daniel says, "that's not how you wipe the counter. Didn't your mom teach you how to clean up after yourself?" They are on their best behavior, eager to show me how adult they are.

Jeff looks at my worried expression and says, "Don't worry. What happens in this house stays in this house." I am worried about the future, and at the same time I am not worried. I know these boys; I have seen them every other day for the past four months. In a way this feels like an extension of our casual, conversation-filled prep-block "class," minus the accounting books. I trust them, and I am confident that this evening will stay a privileged secret among the three of them, or at least that their lack of respect for authority will prevent them from ratting on me.

The weight of perfection is lifted by these boys. Their very naturalness lulls me, and I can forget the enormous trust I am placing in them. The rules and sanctions and protocols of our lives outside this house tonight are temporarily discarded. I feel as if we have lost our skins in a poker game, or left our roles at the door, allowing the persons that we are to step neatly across the threshold. They have accepted me, found me cool enough to "hang" with, given my safe and proper life the gift of excitement and risk. In exchange, they swear profusely, sit on my countertops, feel special because they are the ones chosen to be here, chosen to make pizza with their teacher. I do not reprimand them for their language;

they do not comment on my obvious lack of judgment in allowing them to stay.

I can be myself with them, no perfect front required. I can sit on my own countertops; I can say whatever comes to my mind. It is a tremendous relief: they just nod their appreciation, and sometimes they laugh. I accept Troy, Daniel, and Jeff. I don't see them as "skids" or "badasses," as they are categorized at school. I listen to their opinions and appreciate that Daniel can talk about poetry, that Jeff has a great sense of humor, and that Troy loves animals. I sense that each one of us is closer to ourselves than we are able to be in our regular lives.

"We were thinking," says Jeff, clearly the designated front man, "how can you tell kids that smoking is bad if you've never even tried it? Will you try a joint with us?"

I have already crossed the line, and like a dieter out for a special dinner, I have apparently given myself permission to ignore the usual boundaries. I know that I am doing something wrong, certainly against the rules, yet I lie to myself that I deserve it after years of following every rule there is. I feel safe with these boys. I can say or do anything and they will not judge me. Am I bad for wanting this acceptance, this excitement, this taste of teenagehood, for just one night? I ask myself this question, and answer, No, I am not bad, I am just lonely. Tonight, I am tired of it; I just want to feel good.

We stand out on the balcony. The evening air is cool. I can feel myself coming alive. "Here," Troy says. He holds the rolled white cigarette out to me.

"What do I do?" I ask.

"Just inhale slowly."

I try it and immediately double over, coughing. I have never even tried a regular cigarette. My sinuses tingle. The boys laugh. Troy bends down to me: "Are you OK?" I nod, still coughing. His hand rests warm between my shoulder blades. I think, tonight I am not a teacher.

We settle in for a video. Halfway through, I look up and see that while the other two boys are spread around the room, Troy and I are sitting close, our shoulders pressed against each other. This is fun, the most fun I can remember having in the longest time. At eleven, Jeff calls his mom and then reports, "Daniel and I are going to my place. Sorry, Troy. My mom says only Jeff can stay at our house tonight." Later I find out that this is a setup; they have planned to leave Troy stranded at my house.

As soon as the two boys leave, Troy turns to me as if he has known this would happen all along. It feels natural to be next to him, not strange at all. The room around us is dark and quiet, and the air is suddenly serious, as if we have finally come down to what we both know is the real purpose of the evening. My cat purrs softly beside us on the couch. Troy reaches his hand behind my neck and gently pulls me toward him. A kiss brushes my lips. I say, "We can't do this. I'm your teacher."

"Yes," he says, then kisses me again. His lips feather lightly off mine; we are barely touching.

We kiss as if we are standing on either side of a fence, our hands at our sides, our faces reaching carefully over barbed wire. His touch is so faint that I can almost imagine it is not happening. Yet every nerve in my body is attentive. I feel intensely, forcefully alive. I am not drunk, but my mind does not work in any familiar way. As if I am testing for raindrops, I lift my face and close my eyes. My whole being is focused on Troy's kisses. Reluctantly, illogically, disastrously, and oh so willingly, I let myself kiss him back.

This does not feel like a crisis but like the beginning of a recovery. Yet my body and my brain are at odds. It is so wrong; it goes against everything I have been taught. Troy's eyes are serious, absorbing my hair, my shoulders, my hands. He whispers, "You are so beautiful, so incredible..." He traces two fingers deliberately over my face, which is already accumulating lines on its forehead, under its eyes, and around its mouth. I do not understand why I am risking so much for so little. Maybe I think I can find love. But I know this is crazy. I am short-circuiting.

What is happening, what are we doing? I ask, but Troy is steady. I can breathe for the first time in years. The muscles in my neck release as I inhale great long sweet breaths. Recovery. Madness. I feel like me again.

I sense only close details. The bare plywood floors. The watery blue glow from my computer in the spare room. The smell of fresh paint and pot smoke. Troy's chain cool against my skin. His face pressed against mine. I smell cologne, smoke, toothpaste. The light outside is lifting the sky already. I wonder how many hours we have been kissing.

Strong arm around my waist, Troy leads me in an dance that feels long forgotten. Sex happens, but we are tired by now and it is gentle and mellow, a footnote to our first 5,000-psi touch. I am seeing daylight after years of darkness. In the pink and blue light of my bedroom, the room I share with Mark, I feel Troy's chest rise and fall. He exhales deeply, as if in relief, and with one arm keeps me bound tightly to him. For a few more minutes I will let my body relax against his before my real life begins again.

Resting my head on his shoulder, watching the smoke from his cigarette as it snakes out the window, I feel at peace.

# Morning

*N*INE A.M. My cat is clawing at the screen door. Beside me, a tousled patch of blond-tipped hair and one smooth shoulder are visible. I feel shaken and confused.

I let the cat in and pour coffee into the machine, an automatic motion, just like any other Saturday morning. How will things be between us? I am certain that Troy will want to leave as soon as possible. My quiet house, with its morning silence and the smell of wet grass through the open windows, will be too much for him. He will not want the domesticity I have created with Mark, he will not want to spend time with me, he is not a part of this house or this morning, or of the rest of the day I will have.

At this moment, I am not worried about my career. I am thinking about how old I look in the morning, how the lines under my eyes are so noticeable, how maybe he will think he's made a big mistake. Pressing my hand on his shoulder to wake him, I prepare myself for the rejection that must follow.

One eye flashes open. "Mmm." He smiles at me sleepily, then closes his eye and thrashes the covers around a bit. "I'm hungry," he says into the pillow. Then, turning to me hopefully, "Got any breakfast?"

We eat in silence surrounded by the smell of bacon and eggs. I think of the fifties, and farmhouses, and men who work in the fields. We have no future at this moment, and I laugh inside that I am eleven years older than he, a modern woman, and yet I take pleasure in serving, pleasure in his thorough appreciation of the food.

After a while, I can stand the tension no longer and say, "So . . . how are you feeling about last night?" He is up, walking around, gathering things and getting ready to leave. Today, Saturday, I have to be at the school by eleven to help with the yearbook, so I am also moving and gathering. Even as we work around each other, I notice that he needs a haircut and that there is a trace of car grease under his fingernails. These hands were on my body last night.

He stops, as if he hasn't considered the question. He walks over and wraps his arms around my torso from behind. "Good," he says, his chin finding the socket of my neck. "I feel good about last night." I resist his embrace slightly; I can feel the stiffness returning to my muscles.

"I shouldn't have let that happen," I say. "I'm sorry. It won't happen again."

"I know," he says philosophically. He turns me around and kisses me on the forehead. I feel ridiculously like a little girl.

It is not until I am at school, helping the students sort through text and pictures, that I begin to panic. From my office at the school, I phone my friend Katherine. I am thinking about the rumors of male teachers who slept with young students when I was in high school. I think about my seminar at UBC, where the guest speaker asked us who knew of a student-teacher affair when they were at high school and almost every hand immediately went up. I am thinking about what Robin, my sponsor teacher during my practicum, said about the BC College of Teachers newsletter: that the only thing worth reading was who got fired for having sex with a student. I think about my high school art teacher, whom I loved and who loved me in ways that may or may not have been appropriate.

"I just did about ten bad things," I say.

"I don't believe you," my oldest friend says.

"Oh yeah?" I say, and tell her about last night. I am not worried about telling Katherine—I know that she won't judge me or threaten me with any consequences. She knows I am a good person, and she will try to understand. Our trust with each other is one of the constant blessings in my life. When I am finished, she says confidently, sternly, "It's OK. It was only one night. Put it behind you." She is right. Everything will be OK.

All day I live in a state of panic that does not feel totally related to the events of the night before but somehow seems representative of the extended sense of crisis I have felt for almost a year. The crisis is my relationship, how feeling unloved has made me cling to any sign of affection from any source. My sexuality, almost fully buried, has awakened and whipped itself up around me like a tornado. I am running full speed along an unknown path that will take me to an unknown destination, and perhaps closer to my own truth.

That night at home I wrap myself in the softness of the blanket on my couch and stare out the window. Steam from my tea fills my nostrils, and the cup warms my hands. I feel nauseous. I have cheated on my partner, had sex with my student, put my career at risk. I am shocked at how easy it was to ignore the rules I have lived by for so long. I can't believe I was able to cheat on Mark after eleven years of fidelity. Worst of all, part of me wants to do it again.

By Sunday morning I have almost put the night behind me as simply a huge error in judgment, a one-time thing from which my recovery is imminent. Mark will be home tomorrow, and my life will go forward as normal—because how can it be otherwise?

The phone rings. I hear Troy's voice: "Can I come over?" I am transported back to Friday night. I can't understand why he would want to see me again, but he does.

I say, "It's not a good idea." There is a small window in my voice, an opening, which as an alternate student he is an expert at pushing wider.

"Just for an hour," he says.

I feel the bottom drop out of my resolve. "OK," I say. I tell myself, I will just get one final dose of this feeling, enough to sustain me through the rest of my life with Mark, before I send him away for good.

When he arrives he enfolds me in his arms. We stand that way for a long time. "Do you want to watch a movie?" he asks.

It can't hurt; it's just a movie. We lie on our sides, spooned. The January sun dips weakly into dusk. Around us the basement is cold, and the blue sleeping bag we are wrapped under forms a warm microfiber barrier.

"When does a one-night stand become not a one-night stand?" I ask, to myself as much as to him.

He lifts one of my hands and laces his fingers through as if we are about to play mercy. If we did, I have no doubt that he would win. "The next day," he says deliberately.

I let out a dry laugh. Oh shit, I think, you are so amazing. I love this, love being with you, lying next to you, and I am trusting you so much. Exactly how am I going to have this joy for only one weekend? How am I going to put my feelings aside? I say, "I'm going to get in so much trouble if anyone finds out. I'll get fired, at the least."

"They won't hear it from me," he says seriously.

Oh God. I have put my whole life in his hands. I look into his eyes, eyes that have lied straight to teachers before, eyes that hold a whole life about which I know nothing— and I believe him.

THAT NIGHT TROY SLEEPS at my house again; we want to spend every last minute together. Monday morning we act like a regular couple after their first overnight date, showering and dressing around each other in the bathroom, eating cereal at the kitchen table. I feel self-conscious; I notice the amount of makeup I apply. It feels strange to be naked in front of Troy, and I am acutely aware of my twenty-nine-year-old body. With part of my brain I am thinking about school and how it will feel to be in front of my classes now, with this weekend so fresh in my memory. Will I be able to concentrate? I know I will think about him all day. I cannot imagine what is going through his head.

As we drive to the school together I am not worried about being seen, since I don't know many people in Gibsons, but I get nervous as we near Sechelt. I am extremely aware of the other cars around me. I remember Mark telling me about small towns, how you could tell who was sleeping with whose wife based on which car was in which driveway after shift change at the plant. I am not sure how small this town really is, but I know that on any given outing I will see people I recognize. Troy knows this town much better than I do, and without my having to ask he lifts the side lever and reclines himself low, out of visibility, closing his eyes and leaving me alone with my thoughts. Twenty minutes later, I pull over to let him off at the park near the school. I feel nervous. Troy doesn't seem to; as if this is just any other day for him, he leans over and pulls me in close. We press our foreheads together for a moment. Then he kisses me tenderly on the lips and says, "Have a good day."

I can't believe how casual he is. Yet he has managed to soothe me with his directness. I want to ask him a question, get something from him, reassurance maybe, or a promise, but he gives me nothing, and I let him go with a hug.

I turn back towards the coffee shop for a much-needed shot of caffeine. By the time my car crests the long hill into the school parking lot, he is there, surrounded by friends, smoking, talking.

"Hi, Ms. Ingram," a couple of girls call.

I smile and wave. "Good morning."

Troy looks at me with the other students and lifts his chin in acknowledgment. We exchange a look, and then I gather my bags and walk into the school. There is a sleepy energy to the morning, the sounds of the school getting louder as the buses deposit load after load of students. Lockers bang and kids talk quietly or chase each other around. Students line the sides of the hall doing homework before class. I think about Troy standing outside with his friends as I prepare my notes for my first class.

THE PHONE RINGS the following Saturday morning. I am on my knees in the garden, digging up and separating tulips. I hear Mark say, "Hello?" Again he says, "Hello?" Then the handset clicks into the receiver. Must be a wrong number. Mark joins me out in the garden, laughing at the pool of dirt and bulbs surrounding me.

"How's it going?" he asks.

"Tough work. I'll bet nobody's ever separated these before." He nods absently.

"Who was that?" I ask.

He shrugs. "They hung up."

Mark is already headed for the garage, his favorite place these days. I stand slowly, stretching my cramped knees. "Bathroom break," I say. Tonight Mark leaves for another BC Hydro trip. Mica Dam has a generator that needs to be rewound. He is excited about the three-week trip. I shake out my dirt-covered hands, trying to get some warmth through them. January—only two months until spring, the most hopeful and poignant time of the year.

Inside, I shake out the phone cord and trail it into the bathroom with me, my heart beating faster, adrenaline coursing through my veins. Star 69, caller ID. A synthetic voice says, "The last number that called your line was . . ." My heart makes a tiny leap. First, star 67 to call block my number from his call display. I dial quickly, my thumb covering the disconnect button reflexively, like a foot preparing to brake in a playground zone. Affairs through the miracle of telephone technology.

"Hello," his voice says.

"I have to run," I say. "Mark is just outside."

"When can I see you?" he asks. "Tonight?" His voice is soft, a whisper, although I am the one who needs to whisper. "Please?"

I want to ask questions, check out assumptions, get reassurance, but there is no time. "Mark is leaving on the 5:30 ferry," I say.

"See you then," he says. Click.

It is every bad romance novel, every affair cliché. I feel excited and happy (he called me, he wants to see me) yet guilty for my deception (I am bad to feel this way, think of what I am doing to my partner, my career). I think of Mark out in the garage and then shove the thought from my mind. I hate myself for feeling good, but I hate the possibility of not feeling anything even more. As I return to my tulips, the knowledge that I will get to see Troy tonight makes my work lighter.

{ 9 }

# Gifts

Y FRIEND OONAGH and I are shopping in Vancouver one evening early in February. I wander around the jewelry store, waiting for her to make her purchase at the clothing store across the mall. Running my fingers along the smooth glass of the display case, I am drawn towards a bracelet with strong rectangular links forged in gold. It seems like fate.

"How much is this?" I ask.

"Not much at all," a man's voice says from over the reflective counter. Everything about this store is warm and inviting. The salesman is dark, Italian or Spanish maybe, slim and attractive. He too is warm, fitting perfectly into this seductive environment, where dreams are captured in gold and silver and precious stones.

"Is it for a younger man?" he asks. Does he know something? Does he recognize me from somewhere? I calm myself, realizing that I am not in Gibsons and that his question prob-ably arises from the size or the style of the bracelet. I think about the past three weeks—Troy parking his car down the street and walking up the hill to my house after school, lying in bed next to him between four and six before I have to go pick Mark up at the ferry, enjoying our time together but thinking ahead to remind him to take his cigarette butts with him. I think about meeting on logging roads, making love uncomfortably in his car.

"Yes, he's young," I say, not knowing why I am admitting this to a total stranger, reading something in this salesman's eyes that is comforting. "Too young."

The man smiles and lifts the bracelet from its velvet bed, draping it slowly across my palm. "No," he says, "not too young for you." There is a long pause. He waits patiently, making me feel as if we have all the time in the world, as if I am the only customer he could possibly need to assist right now. "He will look stunning in it," he says, and though he could not possibly know what he's talking about, it is exactly what I need to hear.

"OK," I say. He asks no more questions but carefully places the bracelet in a box, wraps the box in tissue paper, then drops the package gently into a small white and gold bag. I feel enormously satisfied as I leave, but also guilty. Although I carry a piece of the feeling I had in the store with me, doubts accost me as I step from the soft beige carpet onto the cold gray tile of the mall. Will it be too much? Do I already care about Troy more than he cares about me? Will he like it? How will I hide it from Mark? I shouldn't be doing any of this, let alone acting as if this is some love affair I'm having. I want to believe that Troy shares my feelings, but he is still a teenager; I am probably just a conquest for him, a way for him to feel cool. I am probably making a fool of myself.

I feel heavy inside; yet as I swing the bag hanging lightly from my fingers, I know that this piece of jewelry is his, that it belongs to him already. The square links are filled with emotions I can't begin to define; I will let the gift speak for me. Outside, the clear cold air makes my cheeks tingle and flush. This bracelet holds a memory of our short time together and a promise of intimacy. I am merely the messenger.

IN CLASS THE THURSDAY BEFORE Valentine's Day, Troy asks me if I'm going to the Valentine's dance. I laugh. "I'm *supervising* the dance."

That evening the air is charged with youthful energy. When I arrive at the door, I am greeted by a table full of students, all prepared to stamp my hand and direct me to my supervision station. They giggle and tell me what songs the deejay is playing. A group of girls swirls past me in a cloud of makeup and hairspray. The Grade 8 boys also cluster in groups or push and shove each other. Some of them are wearing ties. The older ones, Grades 11 and 12, are divided into two groups—those inside talking to their friends, and the ones outside smoking and talking to their friends. The outside group is cordoned off; the teacher doing smoke pit supervision looks at me desperately, and I signal that I'll relieve her in five minutes.

"Hey, Nicolle, how's it going?" I greet the pretty young English teacher, the darling of the school staff.

"Oh, Heather," she exclaims, looking as if I am her favorite person at this moment, "can you run and grab some tape from the office—you've got your key on you?"

"Sure, no problem." I like being put to use. I love the energy of these nights. Tomorrow my classroom will be buzzing with excitement about who danced with whom.

Deanna slides up beside me and links her arm through mine. "Five months till graduation," she says. Deanna is smart and pretty, with an attitude of "just watch me" that will do her well in the future.

"Got a dress yet?" I ask.

She rolls her eyes to the ceiling and lets out an exaggerated sigh. "Oh my *God,* it's so amazing, but it's so expensive. My mom says she'll pay half."

Suddenly Laura grabs Deanna and steers her towards the bathroom. "Bye, Ms. Ingram! Talk to you later . . ."

I let myself into the office and grab the tape. On my way out the door, I spy Marion, one of the student council sponsor-teachers who has worked so hard to make this dance happen, and I walk towards her. I can see Daniel, a faded cotton hat pulled low over his eyes, glowering. I guess that he is fighting with Kerry again.

Suddenly Troy pulls in beside me, walking with me, looking the other way as he walks. He is wearing the same clothes he wore today in class, but his shirt is open, revealing a white wife-beater pulled tightly over his muscled chest. A black Bogart hat is slanted across his head. He looks confident, sexy. "Wanna dance?" he says under his breath. He doesn't wait for an answer, but veers off quickly as he sees Marion walking towards me, and strides casually into the dark gymnasium.

"Hi, Marion," I say. "Great dance." She smiles tiredly and takes the tape from my hands, ripping short pieces and sticking them to her arms.

A few minutes later I enter the gym, walking around the perimeter of the jam of kids. The music, much of it remixed stuff from when I was in high school, vibrates off the bleachers. "Every breath you take, every move you make . . ." As I stroll through the middle of the crowd mouthing the words, recalling my own high school dances, I am greeted with smiles on sweaty, flushed faces. Beside me a girl suddenly pushes the boy across from her and stomps away. Her words are lost in the noise, but her face is angry. I wonder briefly if I need to step in, but the boy seems to have anticipated her response and shrugs as he moves away. A few feet away Tom and Maryanne, two veteran teachers, are dancing with each other, real dancing, causing the kids around them to stop and look in laughing disdain mixed with admiration.

Troy has found me somehow. I am surrounded by a group of girls and boys, including him, and we are moving in time with the music. As the notes fade and a slow song comes on, a groan rises from the floor. Some kids scatter, others grab their partners and walk onto the floor to sway awkwardly back and forth. Troy steps towards me and lifts my hands. Standing a foot apart, we move back and forth. I look to see if anyone has noticed, but the kids are preoccupied with each other.

This is so stupid; I am so stupid. I wonder what we are doing. I am reminded somehow of dances with soldiers about to leave for war. We smile at each other, at this pretense, which is far too much for the school around us and yet far too little for each other. I want to dance with my boyfriend the same as any other girl.

"Are you busy after the dance?" are the only words he says.

"I should be home before eleven," I say.

"Let me know when you're leaving," he says.

When the song ends, he leans forward and hugs me briefly—friendly, chaste.

From the corner of my eye I see Caitlin, one of my Grade 11s, lift her eyebrows. In her face I see it all clearly. I feel real shame, seeing myself as she sees me. As I step away from this little fantasy, I am confronted with the reality of what we must look like, the danger I am putting myself in, the risks I am taking. Do I really think that because it feels so natural to me that anyone else will see it that way? I leave the gym quickly and retreat to the safety of a group of my colleagues.

Around ten o'clock, Troy walks by me and lifts his eyebrows, tapping his wrist once. I leave the gym and grab my coat. By the time I say goodbye to the other teachers and make my way to the parking lot, he is in his car. When he sees me he drives away. I get in my truck and drive down the long hill. From the side street at the bottom of the hill his car emerges, and he leads me in a twisted route to what is for me an unknown destination. The paved road becomes unpaved, and suddenly he turns his black car into a flat, gravel-covered area hidden by heavy trees.

I pull my truck in beside his car and turn off the ignition. The night is cold and clear, and despite the glare from the streetlights, I can see stars. I am worried about getting home on time, but I am also curious. There is a crisp feeling of excitement in my stomach. Troy gets out of the car and motions for me to get in. I notice with distant distaste the McDonald's bag crunched between the seats and the open ashtray displaying its cigarette butts. He brushes the passenger seat before I sit down, then gets in behind the wheel and backs out. "Where are we going?" I say.

"Not far." He bounces the car up a narrow trail, under a chain designed to keep cars out, dodging potholes expertly. We are silent.

When the car stops we are at the edge of a small hill. From my window I can see not only a thick expanse of stars but the lights from the coastline spread around us. The view is stunning, the ocean dark and reflective, the lights looking as if someone has scattered glitter across the landscape. "Wow," I breathe.

"Do you like it?" he says.

"Of course, Troy, what an amazing view."

"I wanted to bring you up here." He pauses. "Once, my uncle took me in a helicopter all around here. Have you ever been in a helicopter?"

I shake my head. "No . . . Actually, I'm kind of scared of flying. I've been in a little plane before though . . . a Beaver."

"You have to try being in a helicopter," he says. "I thought one day I might be a pilot." It is the first reference to a career I have heard him make. We are silent for a few minutes, looking around us, absorbing the rarity of being alone together.

Involuntarily, I glance down at my watch.

"How much time do you have?" he asks.

"About fifteen minutes."

He lets the back of his fingers fall slowly down my cheek. "This is the most amazing relationship I've ever had," he says, and leans in to kiss me slowly and softly on the lips. I feel stunned and precious. As he moves closer, he lifts something from around the rearview mirror. It has been there all along, but I just see it now. The gold chain glints in the starlight. "Happy Valentine's Day," he says. A small gold cross sways back and forth. I am so surprised and so touched that for a minute I cannot speak. "Is it OK? Do you like it?" he says anxiously. I twist my head towards the window and he fastens the chain around my neck.

"It's beautiful; it's so beautiful." I am almost crying. "Thank you."

He presses the gold cross briefly into the base of my throat with his index finger, as if to anchor it there permanently. It flashes across my mind that he is marking me, possessing me with this gift. Before I get home I will have to take it off and hide it from Mark.

I reach into the pocket of my winter coat and pull out the slim package of white tissue paper, which I have been carrying around with me all week. Until this moment I hadn't known for sure that I would give it to him. I place the tissue-covered box in his hands, and he opens it as if this is no surprise at all. When the bracelet is fastened around his wrist, it looks as if it has been there his whole life, as if it has found its owner. "Happy Valentine's Day to you too," I say. I do not ask him if he likes it. We sit for a few more minutes, holding hands, staring out the windshield. Troy leans his seat back and pulls me beside him so that I am leaning awkwardly across the parking brake. I don't mind. Although I know that Mark is at home, I don't feel guilty. I feel as if he is my parent, and I have to be home before my curfew.

"I need to get back," I say to Troy. He nods and flicks the ignition key forward one notch. The headlights block the distant view of the city in front of us, bringing the dirt and tall grass around the car into sharply lit focus.

"I . . ." No words come out.

"What is it?" he says, turning to me.

"I need to be careful," I say finally. "If we keep going like this I could end up in love with you. That would be bad." I am trying for lightness in my voice, but there is a tremor in it.

"Would it?" he says noncommitally, watching me. I close my eyes and nod to myself. There is a burning feeling around my heart.

Suddenly I feel the need to be home, to be in my own house and my own bed, to see safe and familiar surroundings. Contradictory emotions are tearing at me, making me want to run away and run home all at the same time. How can I even think about risking my home, my safety, for this sweet but temporary respite? Before the consequences come, I still have the illusion of safety, and I have never even contemplated a risk like this before. I think about Mark, at home expecting me. When I walk in I will know where to put my keys. The sheets on my bed will be clean, because I washed them last night; the lights will be on in the carport; there will be the comforting smell of the dinner we had tonight. How I can even think of risking these things is beyond me.

But I don't really believe that I am risking them. This is not a game, but it is not real either; it is a fantasy lived out. Soon I will wake up in my own bed with this night only a dream that makes me smile when I am drinking my coffee and laughing with my friends. I want safety and security and also passion and adventure, but they are mutually exclusive. Can I possibly have both? I am searching for a way to reconcile

myself, to figure out how I got from being a bright, purposeful eighteen-year-old to a confused twenty-nine-year-old
woman with a common-law spouse and a mortgage at home,
parked in a car with a young man with whom she is in love
(might as well admit it) but who is deadly to her career and
stable relationship. My stomach begins to cramp, and I can
feel the start of a headache.

When we reach my truck I sink into its clean interior
with relief. Troy pulls out ahead of me, and I follow him
back into downtown Sechelt. As I turn the truck towards
Gibsons, he puts his palm on the window of his car. I touch
my fingertips to my own window. Goodbye.

# 10

# Roller Coaster

*W*HAT A LONG DAY," I say, sinking into a chair in the staff workroom after eight hours so far on my feet. It is the beginning of March, midsemester.

"And parent-teacher interviews tonight too," Cheryl says, patting her mark book. I envy her, so organized, so on top of things. I feel behind the eight ball this semester, always playing catch up.

"I know—just enough time to update my reports before they arrive." I flick the computer on in front of me and prop my mark book open, ready for a good couple hours of work.

In the gym that evening we are seated alphabetically, with signs indicating our names. Parents check the signs and their children's schedules to figure out which teacher they should talk to next. I am Ingram, Heather, which puts me next to Irish, George, the automotive teacher.

"How's it going?" he asks when the lineup of parents thins and the evening draws to a close.

"It's OK, but I've got a lot on my plate this semester."

He nods and looks at me carefully. "Are you sure everything's OK?"

For a minute it occurs to me that he is asking about something specific. I feel as if I am at the top of a roller coaster, anticipating the long drop below. I nod, "Yes, I think so."

It is after nine by the time I get home. When the phone rings I am standing at the stove, stirring noodles. "Heather? It's George. I thought that you looked pretty stressed tonight and I wondered if it was because of something I'd heard."

I am still willing it to be nothing, still willing there to be something else he could possibly say, because I don't know what I will do with the information I fear he is about to impart.

"Heather, you should know that there's a rumor around the school that you are . . . sleeping with . . . Troy Robertson."

"Oh . . ."

"I have to ask you if it's true."

"Oh my God."

Short, hard breaths come out of me. "No," I automatically lie. "No, it's not true."

"Well, I know that he's a bad kid, and it's possible that he's spreading the rumor himself. I've watched him, and I know he's quite lusty."

"What do you think I should do?" I ask finally.

"Come and talk to me tomorrow and we'll figure something out. I'd hate to see this hurt your career in any way."

"Thank you, George, for telling me. I appreciate it."

"That's OK, you're welcome. We'll talk tomorrow."

The roller coaster begins its rapid descent.

As I hang up the phone, absently letting the spoon slip under the noodles in the pot, I hear the basement door open, a sound I hear about three afternoons a week now: Troy coming through the door from the carport, which is less visible than the front door. I haven't seen Troy all day, but I knew that he might come by late, after my interviews. I walk slowly downstairs, the impact of George's words swelling up inside me. When he sees my face, Troy says, "What's wrong?"

I can't speak, so he holds me against him as tears start to run down my face. I tell him what George has said. "This could be the end of me. It could ruin my career, Troy. We have to stop. I have to end this tonight."

"Let's go upstairs, come on, it'll be OK." He walks me up the stairs with his arm around my waist, and we sit on the sofa in my living room. I can't calm down, and he pulls out a joint. "This will help," he says. He puts the whole joint into my mouth. "Just wet it." I purse my lips around the cigarette as he drags it out from between my lips and lights it. One of his arms is around my shoulders, the other one is putting the joint to my lips. We sit there, silently, smoking.

The pot loosens my tongue. "What is this?" I say.

"What do you mean?" Troy asks.

"Well, what are we to each other? I know I shouldn't ask this question, but I need to know what you're feeling. I've heard you use the term 'fuck friends.' Is that what we are?" I am trying for a light tone, trying to make my voice sound like whatever answer he gives me will be OK.

"No," he says seriously. "No, I have feelings for you."

"What are they?" I whisper, closing my eyes and sending a wish to the smoky air around me. He touches my face, and I read the answer in his fingertips before I hear the words.

"I think I love you," he says. Quiet. "I *know* I love you," he finishes.

It is what I want to hear, what I expect to hear, what I am afraid to hear. I don't know what he means by these words, and whether it is the same thing I hear—I want you, I want us to be together, I want a future with you. "I love you too," I say. The words hang between us.

As if God has kissed me on the forehead, I feel blessed, lighter, beautiful. We try out the words again, to see how they feel, but the fear inside me is still overwhelming. My fantasy is crashing into reality. "I love you. But for now at least, we have to stop." Arm around my shoulders, Troy nods. We have sex then, on the living room couch, for a long time. It has a desperate, last-time quality to it, and afterwards, tired and still stressed from the day's events, I feel with sinking certainty that whatever happens from now on, I will be facing it alone.

THE NEXT DAY I don't see him at all. He doesn't come to my room in the morning with his friends, and I don't teach them in C block that day. He is ignoring me as he promised, but I'm swamped with raging insecurity. When I speak to George he is practical and proactive and suggests I talk to the vice-principal directly. I am doing something dishonest by denying the affair, but I have ended the relationship, I tell myself, and now I'm trying to save my job. I go to the vice-principal and tell her about the rumor and confirm that it is not true, then I try as much as possible to put it behind me.

During the days that pass I see Troy in the background, talking to his friends, walking down the hallway. I feel his presence intensely. I wonder what he is feeling right now. When he catches my eye or nods in passing, the acknowledgment is brief.

Over the next two weeks in class we are teacher and student again, and I hide in my professionalism, remembering how sweet it felt to hear him say that he loves me. I wonder if that's still true. I miss him, but I also feel good about this decision. If we can be strong enough to resist each other, maybe everything can go back to normal. But I don't know if I can be strong enough, and somewhere inside I hope that he cares about me so much that he can't be either.

MARK IS BACK from his short trip to Mica, and we have plans to meet his mother in Kamloops for a weekend of skiing. Anne is small and energetic like Mark, and the three of us usually have an intense time cooking, skiing, and talking. The bonus is Joanne, my single, thirty-five-year-old friend from Quesnel, who is meeting me in Kamloops for a Saturday of shopping and coffee. Mark and Anne will spend the day with his brother's family, a chaotic household including three children under five.

After a day with Joanne I feel restored. We talk about teaching, share our frustrations and successes, and help each other find solutions. In the late afternoon we sit in the living room of the house Anne's friend has let us use and reflect on our lives.

"Your twenties go by so quickly. I feel old already."

"Yeah, and teaching high school strips you emotionally; you give everything you have to your kids; there's hardly anything left for you."

"It's more than just work, it's everything . . . It's juggling twenty things in your brain at once and forgetting how to just sit and be. It's never making time to lie in bed with someone and talk all day. It's detaching from yourself, denying your senses and your emotions in the name of achievement, success, money, respect."

"Yes, yes, and then there's the men . . . Thirty-something men don't seem to get it . . . It's like they're just one-dimensional, not open, you know?"

I nod. "All these TV shows have thirty-something singles just popping into each other's apartments—who has friends like that? Everyone I know is knee-deep in mortgages and careers and barely has time to say hi to a significant other."

We call our conversations "solving the world," and although the talking feels restorative, we never seem to find any lasting solutions.

Around six o'clock, Mark phones me. "Why don't you and Joanne join us at Steve's for dinner?" I look at Joanne and mouth the question. She shakes her head, no, and then shrugs. She doesn't really want to, but leaves it up to me.

"Mark, we're kind of in the middle of a conversation, and we were planning to go out for dinner just the two of us."

"You never want to join in with them," he says.

"Joanne's leaving tomorrow morning, and then I won't see her again till the summer. The kids are so noisy and we won't get to talk . . ." The truth is that I don't like spending time at his brother's place, talking about new vinyl-sided condos and deals on paper towels at Costco. I want to keep talking to Joanne.

"Fine, do whatever you want," he says.

Later that night, after Joanne has gone to bed, Mark and I have it out. I sit on the slippery flowered bedspread in the un-familiar room at Anne's friend's house. I hate rooms like this, ugly furniture and bad wallpaper. I feel stifled and irritated by the heavy bed frame that screams cheap Sears tradition, sacrifice, and shiny family surfaces. Mark is standing across from me, gesturing, working himself up. His words float around me, but they no longer hurt me. I am in a clear plastic bubble. I can see the anger in his face and feel the vibrations in the air, but they are bouncing off my bubble and falling to the ground. His voice gets dimmer and dimmer.

Suddenly I really look at Mark and feel a wave of affection for him. He is a good person. We have known each other for so long, since we were both really just kids. I have helped him struggle through university and now he can do circles around me with the math that he knows. He has taught me about cars and tools and shown me places in Canada I would never have seen without him. I respect him, but I don't feel much of anything for him anymore. It strikes me with enormous force that our arguments are meaningless.

It is past eleven, and we have to be up at six for the long drive up the ski hill. Mark stops his rant and looks at me. "What is it?" he says.

I sigh, and with a deep breath release the information, not really meaning to. It just slides out of me. "We're fighting about the wrong thing," I whisper. Inhale. "We can't keep fighting about the stuff that doesn't matter."

"What?" Mark is suddenly deathly calm. I look at the ceiling, and my voice breaks with emotion. The words escape, never to be retrieved. I am not scared of what he will do to me;

I just know that there is truth to be had from this situation, that maybe the truth will break through some of our pain.

"I've been sleeping with someone else," I say. Mark says nothing but walks over and sits down heavily on the bed beside me. All of his anger has evaporated. He is weighted and very calm. We are the friends we started out as, when we cared so very much about each other's happiness.

He asks the expected questions: "Who?" and "How long?" I tell him the truth. I have come this far; I see a chance that if I can be honest with Mark, let him see what I've come to, we can start fresh, dig beneath the layers of hurt and recapture the intimacy and curiosity we had during those nights talking on his floor.

"Remember I told you about that guy in my accounting class? His name is Troy. Two months; it's been going on for two months. But it's over now."

"He's your student?" Mark says. "I guess that makes sense; your students are the people you're closest to on the Sunshine Coast."

I am impressed at this moment with Mark's compassion, his rational approach. He could rage and scream or hit me, but he does none of these things. Twelve years ago he brought Debbie into our relationship, so this is familiar territory. But I have not been in this seat before. It feels good to have the words out of my mouth. The air feels clearer, like the air after a summer rainstorm that breaks a long heat wave.

We are closer than we have been in years in this ugly basement bedroom in someone else's house. "What do you want to do?" he asks me, and I lob the question back to him like a volleyball.

"What do *you* want to do?"

He is quiet for a moment, then says, "I want to stay with you. We've invested so much in each other; I don't know how to be with anybody else."

I nod, eager now to have the conversation end so that we can sleep a few hours before morning. I know that there are months of hard discussions ahead of us to bring this relationship back to center. I don't know if it is possible, or even if I want that to happen, but I owe Mark the chance to deal with the information I have given him. I feel frightened and alone, yet grateful for Mark's acceptance. Tomorrow, we will ski.

# 11

# Spring Break

*T*HERE IS A SPECIAL ENERGY at school this morning, the last day before spring break, two weeks after our ski weekend. I feel good this morning, energized, and even confident enough to face Troy. I haven't seen him outside of school since the night George phoned me, although I told Troy briefly that Mark knows about him and that we are trying to work things out.

Chatelech's traditional grads-versus-teachers hockey game is scheduled for noon, so morning classes have been shortened. Busloads of kids will fill the arena, cheering for the Grade 12s as they perform their yearly slaughter of the teachers' team. Sally Thicke, the vice-principal, actually plays hockey and has agreed to lend me her clean, female-sized gear. I pick up the enormous bag and the stick and lug them down the hallway to my room.

At the door, Chad and Neil see me struggling with my key and pull the bag from my shoulder. "Hey, Ms. Ingram, how's it going?" Chad says. He flicks the light switch to my room as Neil dumps the bag of hockey gear onto the large table near the entrance.

"Fine, Chad. Thanks a lot, Neil. Now I just have to figure out what to do with all this stuff."

They start digging through the bag, pulling out elbow pads and shin guards and long striped socks. "You see, it's like this," Chad says, and attaches an elbow pad to his elbow. Neil has the shoulder gear on over his sweater and is fiddling with the straps. I am pulling out my books and setting up the room, paying only minor attention to the hockey gear parade, when Troy appears at the door. Chad and Neil immediately stop talking.

"Hi," he says to me.

"Hi," I reply, making sure that I don't look at him too long. The other boys are turned away, and Troy holds my eyes for a minute longer before he sits and starts fishing through the bag of gear.

"Are you playing today?" I ask him.

"Yeah, I'm playing for the grad team. You and your boyfriend going away for spring break?"

I nod. "Nova Scotia, an eight-hour plane ride."

His face registers hurt, or hope leaving, and his eyes are cloudier than I have seen them before. He lifts a black and white glove. "You need to tape your fingers before you put these on."

Nobody else has given me this piece of information. "Why?" I ask.

Chad jumps in eagerly. "Because then you won't hurt your hand when you're punching people out on the ice!"

I put on my best teacher voice, "I don't like violence in sports. Besides, I'll just be trying to stay upright on the ice, not punching people out. And you're on the other team; you're not supposed to be giving me advice."

Troy smiles, and my heart lifts. It is a real smile, joyful, full of something rich and real. "You're right," he says to me, then turns to Chad and jokes, "Better watch what team you cheer for." Chad's smile falters. Grinning to himself, Troy leaves the room.

On the ice, he is a smooth machine. There is none of the awkwardness I see in class, where he fumbles for homework undone. He skates smoothly under all that gear; by contrast I am cumbersome and heavy-footed. His face is flushed, and strands of hair curl and plaster themselves to his forehead. His passes are successful, and he scores five goals. He convinces the referee to let him play for the teachers' team because we are so far behind. He receives many penalties and sits in the box for as much time as he spends on the ice. When released, he threads his way to the puck and then slides it in and under and around the goalie.

We win. As our team cheers its victory, I skate up to Troy, breathless. "Nice job!" I say, pulling my helmet off. He grins and looks happy for a second; we are standing as close as we have been in almost a month. Unconsciously, I move towards him. Immediately he looks around to see who is watching us and then backs up and skates away. Damn, Heather, you can't just act like nothing's happened, like everything's OK. God, I miss him so much.

It is a wonderful day. After I pack my things and say good-bye and eat the last cookie brought in celebration, I remind my students of their spring break assignments and load all my books and papers into my car. I sit in the driver's seat and look around the parking lot. Troy is standing with his friends; his hair is still damp, but he is wearing his street clothes again. I think about how tomorrow I will be terrified for eight hours on a plane, and then with luck will land in Nova Scotia. We're to stay with Daina, Mark's ex-girlfriend, with whom he has maintained a friendship, as he has with all his ex-es. It's a principle that some days I admire and some days I simply don't trust.

Suddenly I notice that Troy is looking towards my car, just looking at me, staring as he has not stared at me in weeks. Stop it; what if somebody notices? I can't help myself; I stare back. I won't see him for ten days, and my chest feels tight and stretched. Troy, I still love you, I love you so much, but we are not meant to be together. When I start my car, his eyes follow me. While the kids around him are laughing and talking, he is still looking at me. I hold his gaze as long as I am able, then turn the car down the hill, reluctantly leaving him behind.

SEAL IS PLAYING on the stereo in the rental car as we drive to Daina's house from the airport: *These things forever change us.* The notes are soft and solemn and lucid, perfect for my mood. Mark has noticed my changing taste in music; I've read that one of the clues to your partner having an affair is that he or she starts listening to new music.

As Mark and I drive through the icy Nova Scotia landscape, I try to be interested in sightseeing, but the experience feels shallow. The ground is still frozen into solid bumps that will melt into slick mud within the month. We see most of the scenery through a film of wind and tiny ice crystals. There are very few cars on the road. At the house, we meet Daina's husband, David, and their daughter, Jenna. Daina and David run a farm with her parents; they all live in the same house in a rural community a few hours from Halifax.

I feel claustrophobic, just like in Manitoba. I spend most of my time reading. We cannot talk in this house; we can't be alone without appearing antisocial. Maybe it is good for me to be out here, because it tells me what it will be like if I am alone. For the first time, I think about leaving Mark, what that might feel like. The thought, which until now had seemed impossible to consider, feels just slightly appealing, something like escape.

Daina asks me, "Do you want to come with me to get some milk?"

"To the store?" I ask.

She laughs. "No, the guy who brings the milk is down at the Carsons' place. Come on, he's gorgeous."

We drive in the old pickup truck down the single-lane road to the Carsons'. Inside, I am greeted by a thirty-something man with longish blond hair. Daina's right; he is gorgeous. "He lives alone on his farm with the cows," she whispers to me. "He won't even let anyone on his farm because they might contaminate the milk. It's the freshest milk you'll ever taste."

I dip my finger into the paper lid of the glass milk container and taste fresh unpasteurized cream for the first time in my life. My senses are screaming, it tastes so good. I hadn't realized how metallic regular cream tastes. I smile all the way home, noticing the clean air and the beautiful old houses.

I am breaking through the insulation and walking on the edge of sensory life.

As the watery sun dies for the day, Mark comes upstairs, where I am lying on the bed reading a novel. He has been reading a book about women's affairs, trying to make sense of my behavior, and the book sits on the night table by his side of the bed. He sits down heavily beside me. He touches me, in a way that is sexual but I try to frame as nurturing. I nestle myself in close. Sex isn't going to solve this. The thought of kissing him makes me nauseous. I want to run, but I don't. I force myself to try to enjoy his touch. If there is to be any hope for us, I must be able to feel close to him. But Mark can sense my reluctance. Our sex used to be passionate and energetic. Now I lie on my back moving very little.

When it is over, we spoon, me around him, and I try in vain to comfort him. I can feel the layers of damage through his skin. I want us to lie here in this position, as if we are in traction, until all the hurts of the years repair themselves. Can we turn back? Can we love each other enough? I try to send him messages through his back. I'm sorry, Mark. I have no self left to give. I need to find it, and I'm not sure I can do that within this relationship. Maybe you're too strong for me; maybe our patterns are too strong. I can't fight for my life and be free to find myself at the same time. As we lie there I can feel his back stiffen.

"I kissed Daina last night," he says, his tone neutral, without turning to look at me. I can't believe how little I care at this moment. Two years ago this information would have crushed me. "I also told her what you've done." I nod and say nothing. I understand that he is hurt, that he needs to talk to people who might understand. Even at this moment, although I have been thinking about leaving Mark, I am still convinced that we will somehow be together. I cannot imagine my life without him.

Later that evening, I call my dad, who is house-sitting for us, to confirm our flight time home. "Everything's great," he tells me. His voice is warm and familiar. "The cats are fine, and there are even tulips coming up in your front yard." Spring . . . I can feel the whisper-light air though the phone line; I can see the bright tomato-red tulips waxy and brave in our front garden. Outside the window in Nova Scotia, the gray sleet sludges on.

"There's just one thing," my dad says. "Somebody keeps leaving rap music on your answering machine. It's happened five or six times. There's no voice, just this same song."

Sitting by the telephone I feel myself grin. "It's OK Dad, I think I know who that is."

"OK, sweetheart, I miss you. See you when you get back."

"Two days, we'll be home in two days," I say.

He has been calling me. He has been calling me. In the window my reflection lights up the frozen exterior. I feel as if I have found a lottery ticket on the street that is worth twenty dollars. A free hit. I am joyful, giddy. I am all the way across the country, and I feel happy.

OUR PLANE LANDS back home on Saturday, and on Sunday Mark and I go skating. It is an activity we do well together, carving ovals around the rink to hollow, echoing music, moving faster as our ankles get used to the thin blades. Mark is better at it than I am. As a kid he quit skating lessons only at

the point where his mother would have had to buy him men's
figure skates; boys didn't figure skate in Thompson.

My stomach is tense as we enter the rink. I wonder if Troy
will be here. I have seen him before at the rink on Sundays, his
body tucked and coiled as he eagles around slower skaters,
then deeply angled as he ekes out tight, smooth corners on
the ice. I am nervous about seeing him again after what feels
like forever, and about Mark and Troy seeing each other.
When I do see him glide onto the ice, I am scared and yet
unwilling to back away from the situation.

"Maybe I'll go over and beat him up," Mark says.

"That's the first time I've heard you sound upset about this."

"I could," Mark insists, ignoring me. "I could just walk up
and punch him, and say, 'There, how do you feel now?'"

Troy avoids any eye contact with me, avoids us gliding
around as a unit. I keep my head low, concentrating on my
skates. Finally, I say, "Look, if you're going to be like this, then
we shouldn't stay here." Mark pushes off ahead of me. I coast in
a straight line to the boards at the end of the rink. A woman is
kneeling on the squishy black matting of the holding area, tying her son's impossibly little skates. I sit on a wooden bench
as far away from her as possible, leaning my head against the
painted concrete wall. It is like an ice pack against the back of
my skull.

"Hi." Troy is leaning over the drinking fountain mounted
against the wall beside me. He is wearing only a loosely but-
toned plaid cotton shirt and dark brown pants, yet his face
is flushed. Strands of his hair are starting to curl in different
directions, and the effect is charming. He smiles at me.
"How's it going?"

I smile back wearily. "It's hard to skate when your knees are shaking."

He glances back at the ice and then leans towards me. "I know what you mean."

We lock eyes for one more second, and then he is gone and Mark is there. He must have seen Troy come over; they pass each other going through the heavy rink door. For a second I'm sure that Mark is going to say something, but Troy evades him and skates powerfully away. "Are you ready to go?" I ask.

I feel annoyed at Mark, yet too tired to discuss or to fight. He sits down beside me and forcefully, angrily unlaces his skates. I feel overwhelmed with guilt and disgust at the havoc I have brought upon us. Sick. Mark has a right to be angry. I have earned this response, and I must endure it. Across the rink Troy is skating gracefully, and I steal one last look at him as we gather our skates and get ready to leave.

# 12

# Breakup

AT SCHOOL, I keep my head down and teach. I am focused and no-nonsense. My students wonder at my businesslike attitude, my abbreviated responses to their jokes, but they pick up my focus and concentrate on their studies.

Days go by when I do not see Troy at all, except in class, where we behave formally with each other. A wall forms between us, as I fall comfortably back into being a teacher and he continues to be simply Troy. When I see him one day talking to a blond girl in the hallway, I feel a stab of jealousy, but I am also resigned: this is right, it is the way things should be. The hole inside me is good, like the virtuous pangs of hunger to a dieter. I take to marking the days since I have slept with Troy in my daybook with a small x. The path to recovery—I am on the program.

After a few more days I am almost numb. It is C block, the second-to-last block of the day. Troy shows up just as the second bell rings, but Daniel and Jeff are not with him. "Where's the rest of my class?" I ask him.

"Daniel's at home, and Jeff's sick," he says.

We sit across from each other and he lays his books out in front of him but does not pick up a pencil. I sort through a stack of papers, but my recent spurt of efficiency means I cannot find anything that cries out for me to finish it. Troy watches me openly, silent. I cannot look at him; I cannot meet his eyes.

Wendy and Christine come into the room, looking for something to do. "Can we use a computer to check our e-mail?" Christine asks.

"I guess so," I reply.

"Hey, Troy," Christine says.

"Hey," he says, then falls silent again.

The silence in the room is heavy, the girls tapping away to their friends on the Internet. Troy sighs, and I finally lift my head and look directly at him, unaware until this moment that I have made a decision. With reckless abandon, I raise my eyebrows and jerk my head to one side. Immediately he folds his books together and leaves. I pack my things and put them in my office. "Sorry, girls," I say to Wendy and Christine. "I'm leaving for a bit."

"Oh, Ms. Ingram . . ." They plead with me, but obligingly walk towards the door.

Outside, the parking lot is deserted; Troy is sitting in his car. I am driving Mark's truck today. I turn the key to start it, and we follow our old pattern down the hill.

In a few minutes, he pulls his car into a dead-end street. I follow him. Without speaking, he gets out of his car and opens the passenger side of the truck. It is the closest we have been in weeks. I can smell him, feel him; he is so close. He reaches one hand out and tentatively pulls me over to him. The movement is a question. I lean my cheek into the rough fabric of his jacket and breathe in his smell. I inhale and exhale deeply. We sit like this for a few moments. His lips are in my hair, not kissing but breathing, tasting. I wrap my arms around him. He kisses me on the cheekbone, and I kiss his neck in return. The muscles in his chest relax against me. "I thought . . ." he says.

"What?"

He exhales deeply and looks at the roof of the truck. "I thought you'd forgotten about me."

My heart feels as if it is breaking. "Oh, Troy," I say. "I haven't forgotten about you." Silence. I look around but don't see anything but the world inside the truck. "I thought you'd have found someone else by now."

He shakes his head once, no, and closes his eyes. Softly, slowly, he says, "I love you."

I nod miserably. "I love you too."

We kiss, and I think my heart will break with longing. I want this boy so badly. I want to feel this way for the rest of my life. I love you, Troy; I can't believe that you thought I could forget about you. My teacher-self dissolves and I am just Heather again. He is so close to me that my skin growls with hunger. He is running his hands down my hair; maybe his hands feel parched for touch the way mine do. We sit like this for a long time, until the clock on the truck stereo reads two o'clock, and it's time to go back and teach my last class.

Still, we are both survivors on our desert island, the only two people in the world.

At the end of classes the next day, Troy brings his friends to my room. It is rare to see them there after school, but it is the Friday before a long weekend; perhaps he just wants to see me. They tell me about their weekend plans; there's a party tonight out in West Sechelt. "What are your plans, Ms. Ingram?"

"Oh, probably work on the house."

All of a sudden Jeff says, "You should get rid of your boyfriend."

I feel his words like a slap, and for a minute I feel a flash of anger. What does he know? He's too young to understand. Yet I recognize that Jeff is just speaking something he sees. It also crosses my mind that Jeff has been primed for this sentence. I answer him sarcastically, "Oh, you think so, do you?"

"Yes," he says. I shake my head, as if brushing off the concept. Ridiculous. My friends and my family would think I was crazy to give up my relationship, my home, and my security for someone so young.

EASTER LONG WEEKEND, 1999. I don't ever want to live through a weekend like this one again. Amazing how the hardest decisions get made, and implemented, in a flash. How once made, they change your life forever, whether they end up being the right decision or the wrong one.

Mark has issued an ultimatum: "If you sleep with him again, we're through." While Mark is out sailing, I spend Saturday morning with Troy, parked in a car in the rain up a mountain, and we have sex, uncomfortably. When it is over I feel weighted and depressed, tired of cars, tired of hiding, tired of cramped quarters and sneaking and lying. The decision to leave Mark comes suddenly. It is just there, ripping my insides apart, tearing up our home, unraveling the whole tapestry of our life together—possessions, family connections, joint bank accounts.

I say to Troy, "I've been thinking about what Jeff said." I am looking for a safety net, however flimsy, for him to save me from the pain that I know is coming.

He looks surprised. He doesn't say that he wants me to leave Mark or offer me anything to help guide my thought process. "I'll be there for you" is all he says, and I know that he is offering me all that he can. He cannot offer me another home to run to, or even the promise of a relationship. Troy does not offer what he cannot deliver, and I have a certain respect for that. I will have a shoulder to cry on, but the decision and its consequences are mine alone. Is that enough?

As soon as I walk in the basement door, Mark confronts me. "Who were you with? What were you doing?" I have an ace in my back pocket, but I don't want to use it. *I want to do this respectably.*

Do what, Heather? What exactly are you doing? I'm fighting with Mark, as usual. No, this is different. You're leaving Mark. I can't be. I don't know how, and I don't want to. But you do, you're forcing his hand. And you can't leave him for Troy. Troy is young, he's unreliable, you have to know that you are doing the right thing leaving Mark, regardless of what happens with Troy. Do you know that, Heather? Do you? Yes. Yes, I have to do this. You will hurt him. No, no, I will save him by leaving. He isn't happy either.

"I don't think I want to be in this relationship anymore."
That is all it takes. The words are out there, a solid presence. I
am unprepared for this. Juli is coming over for dinner. Mark
and I have plans together this weekend.

"Did you sleep with him again?" Mark asks in a monotone.
He is sitting on the dryer in our cold, unfinished basement. I
am perched on his workbench, surrounded by the tools we
have used to renovate our house. Separating out the tools alone
will take hours. I seal my fate: "Yes."

"I want you out of here," he says coldly. All of the feelings
I have been repressing come flooding out. Have I really done
this? There is no turning back. I lose it. I am crying, and the
crying turns to great heaving sobs. I run upstairs and throw
myself onto the bed. The reality is overwhelming. Packing,
moving, not having Mark to talk to when I need him, not
being half of a couple. I twist on the bed in our bedroom, *our*
bed in *our* bedroom. The last time I didn't have Mark in my
life I was younger than Troy is now. Who the fuck will I be
now? How will I get up each day?

Sobbing and screaming, I am scaring Mark with the force
of my grief. It erupts out of me. The sheets are damp from my
tears. Mascara smears the pillowcases. Who will get the pillowcases? Oh, my God, I can't believe I did this. I can't cope; the
whole thing makes me sick. At this moment I don't believe
that I am saving myself. It is over, it is truly over for me, and
I am stepping off the last step into the icy black water, not
knowing how to swim.

Later, calmer, I emerge from the bedroom. Mark sits at
the kitchen table, staring out the glass door to the street. "I
always knew you'd hit me in the head with a frying pan
eventually," he says.

"I'm sorry," I reply. I mean it.

"You're doing a bad thing," he says. I don't know whether he means leaving him, or being with Troy, but either way it's probably true.

"I'm so sorry," I say again.

"I'll never be able to find someone else now, at my age." I nod, just listening. It strikes me that Mark is more upset at the energy required to start building a life with someone again than he is at the idea of losing me. Through my nausea, I realize that I actually like Mark. I recall reading somewhere that people only change when the pain of staying the same becomes greater than the pain of changing.

I lift the phone, call-blocking the number automatically, and dial Troy's house for the first time in front of Mark. I want Troy to know what has happened, and that there is no longer a need to hide anything from Mark. When Troy answers, I say briefly, sadly, "I have to find a new place to live."

"What happened?" he says.

"I've just decided to leave Mark. I thought you needed to know."

"Holy shit."

"I've got to go; I'm sorry." I hang up the phone.

"I don't envy him getting that phone call," Mark says. It is just like Mark to think of how Troy might feel in the midst of all this trauma. There are some really beautiful things about Mark.

I call a few people to explain that I am leaving Mark. My dad is understanding, having seen me struggle for the past twelve years with this relationship. My friend Katherine, married six years, sounds upset when I try to explain that I'm not happy with Mark anymore, that I am not happy in the life we have together. "Happy?" she says angrily. "Who's happy?"

There is a knock on our door, and with a start I realize that I have forgotten to phone Juli to tell her not to come. When I answer the door, she looks fresh and beautiful, her blonde curls brushing the shoulder of her brown suede jacket, her energy reaching out and embracing me. She looks ready for anything, alive, happy. When she sees my face, she reads what has happened immediately, but I say it out loud anyway, while she is still standing on the doorstep. "Mark and I are breaking up." She hugs me and comes in. "Please feel free to just turn around and go home. Nobody in their right mind would want to stay in this situation," I say as we climb the stairs and join Mark at the kitchen table. Juli leans over and gives Mark a sideways hug.

"You should also know that I have been having an affair with one of my students for the past two months," I say, my powers of self-censorship destroyed. I cringe, waiting for the shock and recrimination.

Bless this girl, she has guts. "Actually," she says, "at least three of my clients are having affairs on their husbands right now. So, at this point, I'm not even surprised. It must be something to do with women closing in on thirty."

Mark and I are both aghast. Then he does something that makes me like him even more. With a smooth motion, he leans back, opens the fridge, and pulls out a bottle of wine. When our glasses are half full, we lift them, suddenly back to first-year university, three friends, three individuals with individual lives, sitting around a table sharing something real. "Here's to new beginnings," Juli says.

FOR THE REST OF the weekend, Juli drags me through stale, smoke-stained basement suites until I find an acceptable place—a little cabin in the woods that I can rent in two weeks. I am drained and dehydrated from crying. It hits me in waves. The first wave of grief was the worst, but the mass in my stomach won't move and I still can't eat at all.

On the Tuesday morning after the Easter weekend, I phone in sick. The idea of five hours in front of a class, pretending I'm OK, trying to teach math or answer questions about balance sheets, makes me shiver. I can't do it; I'll break down.

As I pull packing tape along the seam of a box, I check the time. 8:25 A.M. By now my students will know that I have a substitute today, and they will be cheering. A sub— no real work will happen. The word will spread like wildfire through the school. I haven't prepared to be away, so I have dictated a lesson plan to my sub over the phone. She will be in the unenviable position of having to wing it. God, I hope one of my students, Tara or Amanda maybe, will help her out. Troy will have come by my room this morning with his friends in tow, knowing that he's not supposed to, but needing to see how I am. By 8:30 the final bell will sound, and my sub will be taking attendance.

As I am thinking all this, the phone rings. I have a pretty good idea who it will be, and I let it ring. Four, five. Then the answering machine picks up. A few minutes. The phone rings again. I don't answer. I just can't. The ringing stops. I return to my packing, crying, numb.

At 9:45, class change time, the phone rings again. I picture Troy at school, leaning against the wall, the receiver of the pay phone in the school foyer cradled against his shoulder, sending me mental messages to pick up, pick up the phone. I am still in my pajamas and I look horrible, my face swollen and red. After the fifth call, the ringing stops. I hope this means that he has given up, that he's gone to class and is leaving me to my own devices. I will talk to him tomorrow, once I'm stronger.

Half an hour. It takes half an hour to drive from Chatelech to my house in Gibsons. A knock. Oh shit. God, it's him. What is he doing here? I can't see him. I feel awful; I look worse.

I open the door. He is standing there, eyes large, hands hanging lost at his sides. The concern in his face is overwhelming. I feel so bad for putting him through this. He doesn't say anything but steps forward and wraps his arms around me. Then he says, "Thought you might need some help packing."

I am so grateful to have him here. We care about each other so much; maybe, somehow, there can be a future for us.

# 13

# Happy Together

WE ARE STRETCHED OUT on the floor of my rented cabin. Cool late-afternoon light filters in through the large, low windows. Since I moved in last month, I have already seen two deer in the backyard and a small black bear casually eating its way through the decaying fruit in the grass.

"It's nice here," Troy observes.

"Yeah, peaceful," I say. There are still a few boxes not yet unpacked, but the place is taking shape.

Troy rubs circles on my back. I stretch my arms forward on the carpet. "It feels so good to be in my own place, you know?" I say. "I feel like I can breathe here."

Troy nods. Although he still has to hide his car in the bushes and sit silently when I answer the phone, we have found a measure of peace here in the woods. Troy can spend a few nights a week here and call me each day without too much risk. Our lives feel more stable, and we are starting to act less like tortured, time-strapped lovers and more like boyfriend and girlfriend. I still feel stressed every time I walk into work in the morning, but at least I have reduced the number of lies I have to tell by one, the one about which I felt the most guilt—the lie to Mark.

Troy climbs on top of me, eyes lit up. "Can you breathe now?" he says.

I gasp under his 170 pounds. "Not really! Off!" I shriek in mock outrage. His hands are moving down my sides, gently pinching the skin over my ribs. I am squirming, twisting, fighting, giggling under him. His hands grip my wrists as he lobs kisses at me, at my eyes, my fingers, my belly button. Weaving and dodging, I try to jab my hands under his arms. "Ticklish?" We are rolling around the floor, laughing.

It's no use; I am really in love with this boy/man, who brings such sweet playfulness to my days. Much of Troy's charm (and his mother's and teachers' frustration) stems from the fact that he lives so completely in the moment. Each sensation is felt, each feeling expressed. I reflect on the purposeful, disciplined walks Mark and I used to take, striding up hills and planning our investments or debt-payment strategies, arguing about the best tack to take in a work situation.

Hearts pounding, Troy and I lie side by side, looking up at the ceiling. From nowhere, he says casually, much too casually, "So . . . my mom knows about us."

A horrible sinking feeling grips my stomach as I turn my face to him. "What?" It is a statement more than a question, I am appalled, this is terrible, what the hell is he talking about, how could this happen, oh my god I'm going down . . .

He sees the sheer terror in my face, and rushes to explain. "It's OK; I mean, she's cool with it."

I can't believe this, I am scared. "How does she know? What did you say?"

He explains, "We were in the car—she was driving me down to Gibsons—and she said, 'You're spending a lot of time in Gibsons lately. Are you seeing someone?' I didn't say anything, just looked at her, and I guess she read it in my face. She said, 'Does she go to Chatelech?' 'Sort of.' Then, 'Do I know her?' 'Well, yes.'

"'Is it Heather?' she said. And then I said yes. She seemed to know anyway, and I knew she'd be fine with us."

"What did she say?" I ask, trying to imagine Donna's carefully worded questions.

"She said that she's worried about you, that you could lose your job, and I told her that we're being careful. And she said that she's happy I found someone." Troy is completely relaxed, but my face is in my hands, my head is spinning. All night I will replay this conversation between Troy and his mother in my head, adding details and scenery. Of course people will know; it was really only a matter of time.

I feel an enormous responsibility to her and to her son, to care for him, to make sure that she is really OK with our relationship. I hope she doesn't hate me or think that I am wrecking her son's life. I crave her acceptance, but I am scared to seek it.

"I FOUND A REALLY NICE SPOT," Troy says one morning. "It's all covered with moss, really soft." After school he drives me to the spot. We park by the side of the road and begin hiking up the large gray boulders. It is just April, but the sun is already warm and we are sweating.

"Hey, I'm old, what's your excuse?" I tease him.

"I can kick your ass anytime," Troy retorts, and he sprints with his long legs up the hill in a few short bursts. I quicken my pace, enjoying the exercise, the beautiful warm day, the opportunity to be out in nature alone, away from people, and with Troy.

We lie down on the moss, which is fragrant and soaked with sunshine. We make love in the warm spring sun.

Afterwards, we talk sparingly. "Why did you stop playing hockey? You're obviously good at it."

"Too many early practices," he says.

"Oh," I say, knowing that there must be more to it. "But what else was there to do? You're not exactly a star student."

Silence. Finally he says, "I quit hockey when I was four-teen—when Matthew died."

"Who was Matthew?"

"A friend." There is a pause, and then he says, "I remember we came to school that morning and Matthew never showed up. But there were rumors, and everyone was saying that he died."

"How?"

"We were all hanging out at the gravel pit that night. Then we left, but he and this other guy wanted to stay for a while. They were climbing on the piles, just fooling around and shit. I didn't see him for the rest of the night. The next morning we heard this rumor, so we went into Mrs. Struther's office, but she wouldn't tell us anything. We started to freak out, and finally she told us that he was pulled through the chute where they load the gravel for transport."

"My God," I breathe. "You know, I heard this story when I first came to Chatelech—that must have been the year after it happened."

"Yeah," Troy says. "I dropped out that year, Grade 9. I just couldn't handle the bullshit."

The warm air swamps us, we are swimming in it, floating and bobbing in our own cocoon. I wonder if there is more, if Troy will keep talking; it is such a rarity. "That's how I met Sarah," he says finally. "She was Matthew's sister, and at first we were just, like, consoling each other. Then it kind of turned into something more."

I try to picture Sarah in my head. I imagine her as vivacious and outspoken, with a bravado that would be transparent to someone older but attractive to someone so young. "You loved her?" I say.

He nods solemnly. "She was older, right, like eighteen or nineteen, so she didn't want anyone to know she was seeing me. Mostly we just hung out in her room and watched TV and fooled around."

I move closer and wrap my arms around his bare chest. I wonder if he has told this story to anyone else. The skin on his chest is getting goose bumps; the air is turning cool again. After a while, I ask, "So what happened with Sarah?"

He shrugs, but his eyes are cloudy. "One day she just found someone else."

"Someone else?"

"Well, Steve."

"Your friend who moved away. That must have hurt."

He shrugs. Troy is like an iceberg, ninety percent below the water, hidden in icy darkness. I want more than anything to be the person to pierce that darkness.

Since moving away from Mark and into my cabin I have been able to breathe like I haven't since high school. Troy is part of that; I trust him now; he asks what I think instead of telling, directing, and criticizing. What we have feels real, and the rest of the world, Chatelech included, will just have to live with it.

I snuggle my face into his armpit. You are opening up to me a rabbit hole of eat this/drink that adventure, Troy; I only hope I can hang on for the ride.

SCHOOL HAS ENDED for the summer, and Troy is going commercial halibut fishing—long-lining, he explains to me before he leaves. "Wait for me," he says, standing in my driveway as his mother sits in the car with his packed bags. He looks worried. "Please wait for me."

"I'll miss you," I tell him. We hold each other for a long time before he gets into the car. This will not be my first summer alone, but it will be my first on the Sunshine Coast without Mark in Hudson's Hope, the first without a renovation schedule, the first summer pining for Troy. With Troy gone I will have time to think, time to put my priorities in order and figure out how to get out of the situation I'm in. Away from school and Troy for two whole months, I resolve that I will find some answers, and maybe some peace.

The summer does not begin well. I wake the next morning to find the remains of my cat, Teva, presumably ripped apart by a coyote or cougar in the woods behind my cabin. My heart breaks with grief over this little cat with the big attitude. I'm also worried because I've been having some bleeding between my periods. Between crying over Teva and worrying about another biopsy, I struggle with choosing between letting Troy go or letting my career go, the only two options that seem possible. The summer stretches long and lonely in front of me.

A few days later, Dr. Kellett, my gynecologist, phones and says in an unbelievably casual way, "Let's get this over with." I am scared. Scared of pain, scared of more surgery, scared of chemotherapy and radiation, scared of dying. My mind races ahead.

Too nervous to sit and wait until three, I leave early and drive to Sechelt, stopping at the local home store to kill some time looking around. I notice Daniel, Troy's friend, driving a forklift out in the yard, and wave to him. Looking tanned and happy, he jumps off the metal edge of the door and walks toward me. "Hey," he says.

"Hi. How have you been?"

"OK," he says. "You know, fighting with my parents. How about you?"

"Oh, I'm about to go have a biopsy," I say lightly. He looks surprised, concerned, and then turns his head as his supervisor walks by. "Look, I've got to go. But I'll call you after work." He steers his forklift across the yard as I climb into my car to drive to the hospital.

Half an hour later, Dr. Kellett dilates me and inserts a scope. My cervix appears large and slimy on the monitor beside my head. I am holding my teeth together in preparation for the metal instrument that will take a piece of me away for testing. "You know what?" he says. "Everything looks fine; I don't think we need to take a sample. I'm just going to put some silver nitrate in to cauterize a few cells." I stare at the pitted ceiling, screaming in my head with joy and relief.

That afternoon when Daniel calls, I am jubilant and eager to talk. Daniel seems to want to talk too. We end up talking on the phone often. He tells me about the years he has known Troy, the times he has watched his friend struggle with school, drugs, Matthew's death, and girlfriends.

He also describes his disillusionment with their friendship. During one of our conversations, he says, "If Troy and I were driving through the desert on a motorcycle . . ."

"What?" I say, laughing.

"Just work with me here," Daniel continues. "If Troy was driving a motorcycle through the desert with me on the back, and if suddenly we saw a beautiful girl . . ."

"Just standing there in the desert?" I ask.

"Yup, there she is."

"OK," I say.

"Troy's the kind of person who would kick me off the back of the bike and ride away with a girl he's never met before, as long as she was cute, even if it meant leaving me to die of heat exhaustion or dehydration or whatever."

It hits me that this is something I already know about Troy. It also makes him attractive to me. He *is* self-centered and so, in contrast to Mark, meets his own needs and leaves me free to worry only about myself.

I grow to rely on Daniel's calls as a way to talk through my feelings; there is no one else who knows Troy and me as a couple, or who is safe to talk to. I know that after the events of the past months I would benefit from some professional help, but it is impossible, for I would risk prompting a report on our relationship.

"I'll cook you dinner tonight," Daniel says one day in midsummer.

"You can cook?" I ask. Troy does not cook for me. The dinner parties and kill-a-bottle-of-wine conversations I knew with Mark have been absent from my life since March.

"Sure," he says. His parents are in Toronto and we are sitting on the couch in their home looking through his childhood photographs. Each picture has rounded corners, faded 1970s color, and slim, youthful figures with long hair—his parents.

"I have baby pictures at home like this myself," I say, feeling a connection to past that I miss without Mark in my life.

Daniel snips a bud of pot into tiny pieces and presses it down into a thin white piece of paper. We talk nonstop, as if it is a race to get as much conversation in as possible. Daniel's girlfriend, Kerry, is coming over at nine so I have to leave before then. We get stoned quickly.

"Tell me something personal," I say recklessly. He gets up unsteadily, and moves towards the bathroom.

"I'm attracted to you," he says, and disappears down the hall. Kerry is due here any minute. "Are you attracted to me, or am I just a substitute for Troy?" he asks when he returns.

"Yes," I reply ambiguously. At the door we look at each other for a few moments before I get into my car and drive home. We have not cooked or eaten any dinner.

Two weeks later, I call Daniel and invite him to my house for a real dinner. I haven't seen him since his comment about Troy. I haven't talked to Troy in weeks; at night I think about him on the fishing boat and wonder if he is thinking about me. Maybe he has met somebody his own age in Prince Rupert; maybe he doesn't want me anymore. I am beset by fears and insecurities. I realize that I don't really know him very well, that he will never be able to give me the intellectual compatibility I had with Mark. Daniel makes me see Troy in a different light, confronts me with evidence of his selfishness, forces me to question how much Troy really loves me and whether my dream of a future with him is an illusion.

In Troy's absence, I enjoy the attention from Daniel. He reminds me of Mark; we talk about relationships, art, poetry. Although he is young, he can keep up with my thoughts. He also makes me feel desired, sensual. I am still young and, with Troy gone, need a release from the stress of my professional situation. I am concerned only with the glorious present tense.

In my backyard this warm evening at the end of July, we lie on a blanket, staring up at the sky. I relish every sensation, the damp grass, the frog music, Daniel's warm hand on my shoulder. I need Daniel's attention. Troy is not here to make me feel attractive, and the need is addictive, a craving. Ugly stuff. I want Daniel to want me; it is simple, overriding my love for Troy, overriding everything. I am also not yet ready to rebuild the structure with Troy that I took apart with Mark. I am not ready to give my identity over again, be half of a couple. I want to experience things I've only read about, explore my sexuality and power with men.

I tell Daniel about a quote from J.D. Salinger. "Mark found it for me. 'Happiness is a solid, but joy is a liquid.' Do you get that?" I am still looking at the sky.

Daniel moves closer, drapes his arm over my waist. "It means that joy is harder to hang on to, more elusive, I think. But that happiness is something you can touch and feel day-to-day. Yeah, I get it." He leans over me. "Can I have a kiss?"

"Maybe," I say teasingly. I am enjoying the game, the illusory power to say no. "First you have to earn it." I am stretching my power like an elastic band, testing whether it will break.

"OK, what do I have to do?"

"I don't know," I laugh. "But I'll let you know when it happens." He kisses me. It is electric. I don't think about my love for Troy; that is filed away somewhere inside me. This is immediate, selfish. I want this, and I am tired of putting my wants away for the future.

It is getting cold, so we move inside. This is dangerous, because it requires a decision, more than merely moving from one easy moment to the next. Daniel calls Kerry, and I listen while he tells her he is spending the night with a friend. We climb into my bed fully clothed and spoon around each other, awaiting sleep, which will not come. Eventually we make love. It is about 4:00 A.M. when we finally fall asleep. We do everything and anything, as much as we can think of. We are trying to impress each other. Twice he calls me Kerry and is mortified. I laugh, take it as a compliment, and tell him that he is a good boyfriend. Late in the night he gets angry with himself because he can't keep going; we are tired.

Yet I want to keep going, to make the fear I feel about being with Troy go away, to be connected with another human being and outside my own head for those hours. I do not feel guilt; I am already sleeping with a student, already well down a road that will surely lead to my destruction.

What's one more thing? In comparison with what I have already done, being with Daniel is minor. I don't care what anyone thinks. I will use this night as a piece of the puzzle in finding myself.

THE SUMMER IS HALF OVER, and I am no closer to figuring out how to leave the job that I love or what to do for a living instead. The expenses of leaving Mark—a lawyer for our separation agreement, rent and damage deposit on a new place—plus the summer without pay, mean that I need my job. The economy on the coast is small and resource-dependent, with few opportunities to earn more than minimum wage. I feel more trapped in the box I have created for myself than ever, and as September and the school year approach again, I feel a mounting desperation to find a way out.

When I hear Troy's voice through the phone from Prince Rupert a month into his fishing trip, his voice breaks with loneliness. I feel his neediness through the phone, and my heart reaches out to him.

"Do you think you'll get any shore time?" I ask. "Maybe I can come visit you."

"Could you?" he asks.

"I don't know if it's possible, but my friend Joanne is driving back to Quesnel; maybe we can coordinate a drive together and I can catch a bus out to Prince Rupert."

After an eight-hour drive, we arrive at Joanne's new townhouse. I have left her number on my answering machine, hoping that Troy will get to shore in the next few days and call me at Joanne's. When he phones her place early the next day, she is amazed. "You should buy a lottery ticket today," she says. "Luck is with you."

"Do you want to come out fishing with us?" Troy asks me.

"Yes," I say, not even knowing what that means. I have never been on a fishing boat before.

I take an overnight bus to Prince Rupert that arrives at nine in the morning. Troy is there, bleary and rumpled, looking as if he has not slept all night. When I step off the bus, he wraps me in his arms. "You have to have a fishing license to go out on the boat," he says, so we walk to the Fisheries office, where a matronly woman with dyed red hair fills out the forms for me to sign. Troy is hanging on to me, his arms wrapped around my waist as I write. I feel whole again surrounded by him. The night with Daniel two weeks ago nags at me. How could I have not appreciated this beauty I have with Troy? I am filled with self-loathing and disgust for my immature, selfish neediness. With Troy I know I am loved, and when I am with him that feels so much more important than anything else.

Troy's skipper, Les, is a grizzled sixty-year-old veteran of small boats and big seas. He is also a dedicated and generous surrogate father to Troy; he took Troy at fourteen away from the drugs and petty crime of small-town Sechelt and has offered hard work and guidance each summer since. He has known and cared for Donna and her sons since Troy was six years old. When Troy introduces me to Les, I feel momentary remorse for this spontaneous trip. Les sends Troy to pick up their laundry and sits me down in the cabin. "I'm not happy about having you here," he says. I realize that Troy has not prepared him for my arrival but has told him only last night who I am and that he has invited me to spend a week with them on the boat. "I don't like having women on board. Troy's here to work, not to socialize. And if you get seasick, we're not running back to port."

He is abrupt and unfriendly, with good reason. I feel like crying but manage to hold myself together. Wondering if I should simply jump back on the bus and go home, I say, "I will do whatever you want me to do. Just put me to work." Les looks surprised. I am eager to prove myself to him, to show him that I really care for Troy and will pull my weight over the next week.

That evening, as we motor across the smooth sea to our anchorage in the beautiful Queen Charlotte Islands, I cook dinner and pour Les's homemade red wine into three tumblers. Strains of jazz float from the cabin. Troy shows me how to punch large hooks through chunks of frozen salmon and then lay the hooks in a bait box so they won't tangle. The sun sets on the dimpled water. A fish jumps and lands with a splash. I laugh out loud. "Why do they jump like that?" I exclaim.

"They're happy," Troy smiles.

We are happy too, so happy, and the stress of the summer and the school year fades away. Watching the leaping fish, drinking wine, we listen to Les talk about his youth hitch-hiking across Canada. We are three generations talking and laughing, and the evening is special. Working beside Troy as the sky deepens, I feel content and completely peaceful. Now I know why this has all happened. I feel as if I have found the love I have wanted all my life.

The next day Troy rolls out of the bunk at 4:00 A.M. The ocean is oil-slick calm, perfect for fishing. I get up early with the men, passing coffee with a shot of scotch out to Les and cooking toast and eggs for their return to the cabin once the first line is set. After he has eaten, Les nods his appreciation for my efforts. With gruff thoughtfulness, he finds me a spot where I can brace myself against the rolling swell of the boat and take black-and-white photographs. Troy bends and lifts in his checked jacket and green rubber overalls. He pulls in a halibut that weighs as much as I do.

"That's the biggest fish I've ever seen!" I exclaim as the 120-pound fish is subdued on deck.

I love watching Troy work, the tight, automatic motions of setting and checking the line, the anticipation of catching something with each moment, and the sudden excitement of a struggle with an enormous fish. In the evenings, Les and I watch Troy scrape out the guts and clean the fish before he tosses them down the long chute into the ice hold. I ask question after question about the boat, the equipment, the different types of fish, and Troy seems proud and happy to show me his expertise.

When the week ends, Troy and I spend a night together on shore before I must take the bus back to Gibsons. Our time together has solidified our relationship as I never thought possible, and I feel that we have a future together. I know now that we really love each other, we can be whole together, honest, handle anything. My optimism is blinding.

"Troy, there's something you should know," I begin. I try to explain about my night with Daniel. "It means nothing; I'm sure about us now," I say, certain that he will understand. We feel so strong together. As he pulls me close and holds on to me like we are perched on a ledge about to fall, I feel tears spread from his eyes across my cheeks. "I acted like a selfish, immature idiot, Troy. I'm sorry," I say. I pull away to look at him but he buries his face against my shoulder, not speaking. The tears come faster.

# 14

# The Last Time I Am a Teacher

WHEN SCHOOL BEGINS in September, I think only of coping for one last year before I can get out. My goal is to survive. To accommodate the school's schedule, I have agreed to forgo my prep block this semester, in exchange for two starting in February, so I am going to have to be on top of curriculum, class management, and marking.

Troy has spent the last two weeks of summer in Arizona visiting his dad for the first time, and I have seen him only twice since his return—although he is affectionate, as usual, when we are together. I have promised him that I will never cheat on him again, and I intend to keep that promise. Once, he mentions that he wants to beat the shit out of Daniel, but I hear nothing more about this, and my attention turns to my classes.

Vivian, a fellow teacher and friend, and I have lunch and chat about leaving the Sunshine Coast; we both find the place claustrophobic. I tell her that I want to make it through this year as a teacher and then look for a new career. I really believe that it is possible for me to move through this experience and into another career without an enormous crisis. The consequences of failure are too horrible to contemplate.

I make it through my first week, but I feel panic and dread when I am in the school office. Nightmare—I didn't know how hard it would be to come back to the school after this summer. Every payday feels like a victory. At the same time, I enjoy teaching, like the kids, love my room, and enjoy my classes.

My teaching schedule is brutal. Seven different courses, in one case three courses in a self-paced split class in one room all at once, a new Math 10 textbook, thirty kids in each class. I am at school by 7:15 A.M. and have kids at my door for math tutoring by 7:30. I make coffee and tutor while I set up for class, always juggling at least three things at once.

The regular kids are easy, generally well-behaved with good homework habits. My thirty-one Math 10 alternates are another story. They fall into three groups: the severely learning disabled, mostly sweet kids who are often tutored one-on-one by the two teaching assistants, who are godsends; the behavior problems, who swear, yell, throw things, leave the room; and the quiet but mathematically challenged, who, unfortunately, tend to get overlooked, as the behavior problems demand most of my attention. I love them all, though. I love my other classes too, despite the fact that I have a four-inch stack of marking and prep at the end of each day.

Things are deteriorating with Troy as he copes with my revelation about Daniel. He is skipping more classes, smoking more pot, hotboxing or driving his new car fast through the school parking lot. The money he made fishing in the summer hasn't even lasted the month. When he comes to my house two or three evenings a week, parking his car behind the bushes, we make dinner and sit on the deck looking at the stars. More often now we spend our time arguing about his school performance or drug use; I am beginning to sound more like his mother than his girlfriend. I begin to worry that he won't be able to graduate, that he won't make it to the end of the school year as I have planned.

He is growing farther and farther away from being the attentive, sweet lover with whom I spent a week in August. I begin hearing around school that he is seeing someone, or at least making moves in that direction. When I ask him about it, he denies it, insisting that we are still together, that he still loves me but is just "having some fun." Underneath his nonchalant exterior, he seems angry and hurt.

I also know from teaching him the previous September that he works hard during the summer on the boat and has trouble concentrating and doing schoolwork when he returns to school. He has friends, he has money, and he is eager to party. By contrast, I am desperately focused on helping him graduate and on getting through this year with my job intact.

The rumors that started last year are back. Troy and I rarely speak to each other at school, and barely acknowledge each other in the hallway; he has even transferred out of my Accounting 12 class for an English class he needs in order to graduate. Still, snatches of conversation drift by me: "I hear that Troy is sleeping with Ms. Ingram." "Oh, that rumor's old, man." Some kids believe it; some don't.

One day during lunch, when I am tutoring Meghan in her Math 10 correspondence course and grabbing bites of a sandwich, she says to me, "You can relax with me, Ms. Ingram. I know your secret."

"What are you talking about?"

"I'm seeing Jesse, Troy's older brother. He told me. Don't worry; I don't have a problem with it. It's nobody else's business." Jesse, who had graduated two years earlier, had told her after she noticed Troy's frequent absence from his home.

Events are getting away from me. Too many students know, and I fear that even some of my colleagues have heard the rumor and suspect something. To avoid any questions, I spend less time with other teachers and less time in the staff room; I don't have any spare time anyway.

I hear through the grapevine that Troy is planning to assault Daniel, although he promised me he would not. During the fishing trip in August, we talked about getting married one day; now, in October, he calls or comes to see me once every three days. I am grateful to him for staying silent about our relationship, but I am aching inside that he does not seek out my company as he did before.

I begin to wonder if all the risk is worth it, if there will be anything worth having with Troy once we make it through this year. I feel so impatient. I want so badly to believe that he loves me. But he no longer says that he wants to be with me forever. My heart hasn't changed; I love him, and I don't want to lose him. But I have so much at stake that it keeps me awake at night. By contrast, he seems to have little to lose.

I feel close to tears all the time. I had no idea this semester would be so hard. When I help Laura with math after school, I think about Troy. When Tony refuses to turn his Discman off in class, I send him to the office instead of finding a way to deal with the situation myself. I feel guilty about compromising my position as a teacher and afraid every day of being called to the principal's office to be confronted with the rumors spreading through the school hall. I am afraid of losing my job and my paycheck, since I don't have Mark's help anymore. I am afraid of losing Troy, and I am afraid that he will assault Daniel, which will be my fault. I dream that I am being buried under a ton of slippery fish pouring down from the sky.

IT HAS BEEN THREE DAYS since I have spoken to Troy, and at last I decide that I will confront him about our relationship. Even if things go badly and we end it, at least my stress will be over. Going to sleep that night, I promise myself that I will deal with everything tomorrow morning.

At one o'clock in the morning, the phone wakes me. It is Troy, his voice filled with drunken emotion. "I'm at Brian's. Can you come and get me—please?"

I struggle to free myself from sleep. "What's wrong, Troy? What's happened?" I wonder what has prompted him to call me tonight, why he sounds like the loving, open person I know again. "I'll come get you," I say, grabbing my keys and, without thinking, getting into my darkened car in my pajamas.

When I arrive at the place where Troy has told me to meet him, Troy's friend Brian walks him down to my car. I see and process many things at once. Troy, incredibly drunk, and limping—there is something wrong with his leg. Brian doesn't look surprised to see me; he must know about us. Troy must have told him; who else has he told?

"What happened?" I ask Brian.

Troy mumbles something incoherent about a deer and a knife. Brian folds him into the passenger seat of my car and says, "I took him to the hospital; they put some stitches in there."

I say, "Are you going to say anything about me?"

He shakes his head like that is a ridiculous fear. "No way. Take care of that boy," Brian says, and closes the passenger door.

The whole ride home Troy is silent, but I feel that he is somehow back to himself again. Leaning his head on my shoulder as I drive, he shows me the long knife wound stitched up in the muscle of his calf, and then wraps both his arms around my right arm and pulls himself close to me over the gap in the bucket seats.

All my senses are alive at this moment. I do not confront him as I have planned. Dimly, I sense that he has come through something significant and needs me right now. As we pull into my driveway, he says, "I got kicked out of school today."

I carefully blot the dried blood on his leg with a warm washcloth, then give him two aspirin and help him into my clean, warm bed, where he falls asleep almost immediately. I can feel a crisis coming. In the meantime, I am only responding to each event as it occurs. I lie beside Troy, my mind drifting back.

I remember my dad taking us to see my mother, hospitalized for her manic depression, and the clay figurines that she would proudly show to my sister and me. I would throw them out, destroying the evidence of her fragile mental health. I wanted to be like my dad, logical rules and routines, competent, safe. I wanted to be strong enough not to need her or miss her. I fear that I am just like her. Everything I did, my marks in school, living up to any standard that was set for me, was to prove I could succeed without her, that I was strong enough. And I did. Then, when I couldn't live up to Mark's high standards, when he chose Debbie over me, total devastation. I never recovered, even though I won him back in the end, even though I have my mother now as a wonderful friend.

I am going under. It started out simply. I needed love, and I found it in Troy. I do love him. But now I have messed everything up; I slept with Daniel; I have hurt him and betrayed my other students. I don't know what to do to make things OK.

I sleep restlessly. The next day, Troy comes by my house after I get home from school. We make love and lie in bed closely, not speaking. Now that he has been kicked out of school, he hangs out in Sechelt with his friends during the day, sitting at the gas station, smoking cigarettes, talking.

Finally, a week later, a break. Friday is a professional day. In the morning we have presentations, and I relax into the presenter's voice, allow myself to fully be a teacher again for one day. It feels so good just to be able to focus on my job. Around me the school is quiet, with only forty people instead of eight hundred. The halls echo, and the custodians take the opportunity to polish the floors. I look at my classroom, still a place of discovery and learning, and I feel real guilt for my actions. The empty room with its student ghosts reproaches me. *Ms. Ingram, what about us?*

At lunch, I seek out Vivian. She has to go pick up her sister from the ferry, so I go with her for the drive. I have sat in her minivan many times before, including the night she told me about her family's problems, her abuse as a teenager, her struggles with alcohol. We have shared stories, but we always seem to stop just short of being good friends. She is an enigma, closed in her emotions, but rational and always professional, and I trust her judgment. Surely, Vivian will know what I should do. I am at the top of a ladder that is running out of rungs. I take a deep breath, and with the feeling of stepping off the edge of a cliff, I ask her for help.

"I need to talk to someone. But I also need you not to tell anyone. I've been sleeping with Troy Robertson. And I love him, but things are going badly, I'm stressed, and I don't know what to do." My voice is choppy, miserable, stilted.

Vivian raises her eyebrows, but does not look overly surprised. "Yes, I figured something was going on; I'd heard the rumors."

"What do you think I should do?"

"Well, he got expelled from the school, didn't he? So there's not even an issue anymore—I wouldn't quit your job yet."

I know that I am putting her in a difficult spot by giving her this information, but it does not occur to me that this conversation will ultimately bury me. I am thinking only of salvation. Please, talk sense, be rational, and I will absorb it and be rational too. She asks me questions, about Troy and our relationship. At one point she says, "It sounds like you two have something really beautiful." But then she starts talking about another teacher she knew who took some students on a week-long field trip and was accused of having sexual contact with one of the girls. "Heather," she says, looking directly at me, "they *buried* him." I go cold. This situation will not get better. I realize I have just made a mistake. Dread envelopes me. Help is impossible now.

On Sunday, Vivian calls me. "Can I meet you for coffee?" she asks. "We need to talk."

Battery acid fills my stomach. I arrive early, but I can't sit still for coffee, so we walk down to the beach near the school. It is a beautiful October day, with blue skies and white clouds, the ocean rushing and crashing industriously against the gray sand.

"I've spent the whole weekend drinking and thinking," Vivian says. "And I've decided that I just can't risk my family's safety and all the things that I've worked for. If you don't tell Bruce Jansen yourself, then I will have to report you." Betrayal, knives and stones. I am destroyed. I never want to see Vivian again. Fine. Fuck you. You won't help me, I'll destroy myself further. Watch me, enjoy this, Vivian. Here I go.

"Don't ever speak to me again," I say to her, and walk away, back to the coffee shop, where I look up Bruce Jansen's phone number at the counter.

Bruce looks surprised to see me on a Sunday, but he welcomes me into his home. His wife gives him a questioning look, but she smiles at me as we move into the kitchen. "Is this private enough?" he asks. I shake my head, "No."

Outside on his deck, just the two of us, I look towards the water and take a deep breath. There is a rope pulling me forward and I am doing the only thing I know how to do, be as honorable as I can at this point. There is nothing to do except take my punishment.

"I am here to resign," I say.

"Why?" he asks.

"I've been having a relationship with a student," I say for the second time in three days. "Do you know who it is?" I ask him.

"No."

"Troy Robertson. There's been a rumor for months now. Vivian knows, and some students know too."

The words do not get any easier to say. My voice is shaking but I am calm. Maybe some good can come from this. It feels good to be honest at least. Finally, I am an honest person, a good person—I believe this still—and I tell Bruce to the best of my ability what is my truth. "Yes, I love him. I know it's wrong, and I know that I need to leave the school." Strangely comforting, this man; he is compassionate. "I would like to say goodbye to my students," I whisper miserably.

He murmurs something about getting a substitute on Monday and lays his hand on my shoulder. He does not tell me that everything will be OK, because it won't. But I feel at this moment that I am doing what is right, that maybe I will be fine after all. I do not know that I will never stand in the school where I have worked for four years again. I do not know that I will not see my students or stand at the front of the classroom again. My things will be delivered to me, picked up by someone else.

It never occurs to me to keep lying, to allow Vivian to make her report and to deny it. It does not occur to me to call my union representative and try to protect myself, or to fight to keep my job. I need this stress to end. I see the top of the ladder, and after that, only sky. I want to punish myself for being so weak. I hate myself. I have been selfish and unprofessional. I can hear the voices of the people around me. I can hear the shock and the disbelief. Not Heather, she's a perfect student, well-behaved daughter, devoted and effective teacher. All along I have known that I am not good enough. Nobody else can see how hard I try to be good and yet how ugly I feel inside. I hear Mark's criticism, my dad slamming his fist on the table when I am late for dinner. I am wrong. I am bad. I need to give up my life. I don't deserve Troy. I don't deserve to be a teacher. I don't deserve anything good.

WHEN I LEAVE Bruce Jansen's home, I am walking in a nightmare. I don't know what to do next. Almost four o'clock in the afternoon, the sun is still shining, and the ocean glints behind me. My car seems to drive itself towards Sechelt. Maybe I am looking for Troy, or for someone else. Maybe I will simply keep driving. When my car stops, I am in Troy's mother's driveway. Standing at her door, she looks at my face and says, "What's wrong?"

"It's over," I say, and then realize that she thinks I mean that it is over between Troy and me. "No, I mean, my job, my career, it's over. I just resigned."

She takes me inside, and we sit in the sunny window of her trailer's kitchen. The last time I was in this kitchen was with Troy, just before Christmas last year. Then I was still a teacher. Friday when I left work I was too. Today, suddenly, I am not. I tell Donna my conversations with Vivian and Bruce Jansen.

"Why did you tell anybody?" she asks in disbelief. "Why did you trust Vivian?"

I can give her no answer that makes sense, though I felt that I knew what I was doing when I was doing it. I try to explain—alone, I felt alone, needed help, did not know where to turn. She shakes her head. I sip the sweet, milky tea in front of me.

I am not Catholic, but there is a power in confession. I must confess and seek redemption. My family and friends will know eventually, so they must hear it from me. I make the easier calls first. My sister, Juli, Joanne, the ones who already know about Troy. Then it gets harder. I call my mother, then my father. I don't even know how to disappoint them in this manner. At twenty-nine, I have never done anything less than bring home perfect report cards, give them good news. "I've been having an affair with one of my students. I told my principal, and I've resigned my position." The words hang in the air. My mother says, "Oh, Heath," in a sad, almost defeated kind of way, as if she has been expecting some kind of bad news all her life, and here it is. My stepfather gets on the line with her. "If there's anything you need . . . ," he offers compassionately. In the background, I can hear my mother's breathing. "We love you a lot," she says.

By contrast, my father's voice is immediate and strong. "What the hell are you doing? How could you do such a thing?" His words are so harsh, so angry, as if I am ten years old and have shoplifted from the local store—except that I never did anything like that when I was a kid. At my high school graduation, I walked around the grad party with a glass of 7-Up and ice, letting the other kids assume I was drinking straight vodka. School was my life, and then Mark became my life. *I don't even understand it myself, Dad. I just needed so badly to feel something again.*

I bring myself back, tighten my stomach muscles, and say tensely, thinly, "I know that I screwed up. Right now, I need your support."

He is quiet for a moment. I know that it is taking everything he has not to lose it with me completely. His love for me is
fighting with his pride and his sense of right and wrong. Finally,
he says heavily, "I'm sorry. Of course you have my support."

When I am finished making phone calls, I sit on the couch
and stare. I have no emotion left. There is nothing at all left
for me. Outside the light is fading, a dusky October night.

I still have a home, but with no job, for how long? I wonder
whether I will have to live on the street, and remember how
Mark and I used to leave our pop bottles on the edge of the
dumpster so that the homeless people who scoured it hourly
would not have to dive inside. I try to imagine myself on the
street, living for day-to-day survival, disgraced. In a fog I put
on my shoes and a big jacket that belongs to Troy. I rummage
through the shelves where I keep tools and where Troy has
dumped some greasy car parts. A box of razor blades from
Mark. I remember him showing me how to get stickers off a
glass windshield with a razor blade.

It's getting colder outside. I tuck one of the blades into
my jacket pocket, thinking nothing except that its presence
is somehow comforting, a glimmer of escape and redemption. I drive down to the beach and sit on the cold concrete
retaining wall, watching the moon light the waves in frosty
peaks. Drowning is supposed to be an OK way to die. I wonder if it will be peaceful. Better than blood, but then I've got
that as a backup.

My eyes follow the ocean as it swells and moves in front of
me. I wonder if I can hypnotize myself and then just walk in.
The blackness looks almost warm. Soothing dark, filling my
lungs. Soothing blood, my own blood, I want to bleed. No more
thinking. Just black. Maybe heaven is just black. It will be

better than facing the people I've disappointed. Bruce Jansen's compassionate but stern face rises before me. My father's voice echoes in my head. Mark, Donna, my teaching colleagues, my students. I am a coward. It will all be better this way.

I am not wearing a watch, but I guess that I have been outside more than two hours. My body wakens me from my reverie when it starts to shake, protesting the cold, damp air. If I stay here, I will get sick and perhaps die, whether I want to or not. And I guess that I do not, because I am still sitting here, and have made no move to walk into the ocean.

My car is driving again, this time to Kel's, only a few blocks away. The alternate teacher at Chatelech, he is as close as I have to a real friend at the school. I have been in his house many times for social evenings. Tonight he takes me in and puts a glass of wine in my hand while I tell him what has happened. Crackling fiercely, the flames from his fireplace warm me.

"Does Troy know where you are?" he asks me.

"No."

"I'll bet he's worried."

"Yes," I say, considering Troy for the first time, "he probably is."

Kel is treating us like a couple, taking me and my relationship at face value. Of course: if you love someone, they will be worried about you. Somehow this small bit of acceptance brings me back to life. "You can use my phone if you need to," Kel says.

I check my messages. There are twelve, all from Troy, all sounding progressively more worried. Around number seven he says, "I just talked to my mom and found out what's going on. Where are you?" After that, he just hangs up each time. I don't call my own house, because although Troy has a key, he knows not to answer my phone. I realize that my whole life is about to change, and being public with Troy is suddenly possible.

Kel sits with me a while, then drives me home. When I step through the door of my house after midnight, Troy is there, asleep with his clothes and the TV still on. The entrance to my house has a vinyl area for mud, and when my shoes hit it Troy wakes and walks towards me. Home now, my knees give way and I collapse into him and onto the floor. "It's going to be OK," he whispers.

"No, it won't," I say.

He kneels down and presses his cheek against my neck, squeezing me tighter. Again he says, "It's going to be OK." With eerie intuition, he pats my pockets and pulls out the razor blade I have been carrying all evening. "You don't need this," he says softly, putting the blade into the back pocket of his jeans.

Even as I am crouched on the cold floor of my entranceway, I believe that the worst has already happened. The hardest part is over; I have finally done the right thing. The lies have ended; I can finally tell the truth, finally live without the fear of people finding out, of losing my job. After ten months, Troy and I can begin to have a normal relationship, although I wonder if he will stick around now that he has left school and I am no longer a teacher. Still, there is a feeling of completion, of putting your hand to your head after your car has rolled into the ditch and realizing that you are still alive. I am alive. I will lose my job, my career, I will miss everything about it, but I will finally be able to say that I am not living a lie. Things will get better from here.

# 15

# Fugitive

*I*N THE MOVIES this would be where the music suddenly intensifies. The next morning I get a call from Nancy Brindley, who is president of the Sunshine Coast Teachers' Association and a former colleague. Her voice is full of sorrow. "Oh, Heather," she says. "I was so surprised to get a call from Bruce Jansen last night. I think we should get together as soon as possible. Can I come over this morning? There's a number of things we need to deal with."

Meetings and meetings. The machinery of school protocol has chunked into gear and is now relentlessly moving forward. It is as if I have stepped onto an exercise treadmill that has started moving underneath me and my feet are moving forward just so that I can stay upright. When Nancy arrives, she briefly explains what the procedure will be. I am OK until she says, "You should know that there is the possibility of criminal charges."

"What do you mean?" I ask.

"Well, in a typical case, the student or his parents would be able to file a civil suit against you for damages, and usually the British Columbia Teachers' Federation would provide a lawyer to counter that suit. But it doesn't sound like that's a possibility in your case."

"Troy and Donna are both supporting me totally," I say.

She nods. "I understand from the lawyers that you can be charged under the criminal code regardless of whether they are supportive of you or not."

I am completely ignorant of the law, and I can't believe what I'm hearing. The tips of my fingers start to tingle with fear, and I have a soon-to-be-familiar sinking sensation. A criminal? How could that word apply to me? In high school, I would have been voted most likely to succeed, not most likely to get a criminal record. I have voiced harsh disapproval of "criminals" my whole life. They are bad people. They murder and steal, are uneducated and deviant. I roughly shove these thoughts from my mind.

Within an hour, Nancy is driving me to the school district office. I am grateful that she is driving; I don't believe I could operate a car right now. Although there are only three of us, we sit at an oval table in the large boardroom, which has been reserved for this meeting. I have been in this office for meetings before; it is where I had my interview with the assistant superintendent when I was hired almost four years ago. The atmosphere is different today.

Clifford Smith, a short, heavyset, balding man in his fifties, enters the room majestically, seating himself at the head of the table. Nancy says, "I have instructed Heather not to say anything."

Clifford nods and begins. "I understand from my conversation with Bruce Jansen that you have been having a relationship with a student at the school in which you taught. Is that correct?"

He is determined to ask me questions anyway. I nod, and Nancy shoots me a look that says, "You don't have to say anything else."

Clifford continues, "Then as the superintendent, I have no choice but to suspend you from your teaching duties, effective immediately."

He hands me a letter, which I read. I feel a wave of disbelief. The letter informs me that I am now considered a danger to all of my students and am suspended from teaching. It names the section of the School Act under which I am being suspended and notes that the district and the police are launching separate investigations.

I feel sick to my stomach. What could they need to investigate? I was honest. I finally admitted to this relationship and am trying to do the right thing. Honesty is the best policy—isn't that what we teach children, what is said over and over in times of moral quandary? And he thinks I am a danger to my students, the students I love, spend hours helping, coaching, and mentoring. Dangerous? I could never hurt my students like that; I could never hurt Troy like that. Oh my God.

On Friday, if asked, Clifford would have had nothing but good things to say about me as a teacher. Now, three days and one fateful conversation later, I am a menace. I have been judged and condemned. Serious sex offenders have taught in this school district before, and I wonder if Clifford was in charge when Robert Noyes, convicted of molesting many young children over the years, was caught.

Things are moving very quickly. Nancy leaves the room to make a photocopy. When she is gone, Clifford stands and looks at me for a full minute. Then he says sternly, "You are doing the right thing."

I am concentrating on holding back a flood of tears. "Thank you" is all I can whisper.

The following week is a blur. My next meeting is with a lawyer. I wrap myself in a suit jacket and black dress pants— my armor. Alan Black, the black-haired labor lawyer hired by the BCTF, leads me into a small, paper-crammed office with an expansive view of the city. "Tell me everything," he says. "Don't leave anything out." He tells me about something called lawyer-client privilege, and I realize that everything I think I know about lawyers (evil, money-sucking, sharklike creatures?) comes from television. I tell him how I met Troy and what has happened with us since January.

Alan sighs deeply and says, "From an employment standpoint, there is nothing I can really do for you." Then he advises me not to formally resign yet. He will try to extend my suspension for as long as he can. Clifford Smith has led an eight-year battle against another teacher, Bob Bjornson, who was dismissed for misconduct, and he is not likely to back away from giving me the same treatment. It is likely that I will be dealt with as harshly and as publicly as possible. There will be no old-boys-club deals, no silent transfer, no covering up or pretending that this never happened. Clifford will try to use me as an example. As I stand to leave his office, Alan shakes my hand and says the words I will never forget: "You need to get yourself a good criminal lawyer." He hands me a plain white business card, which reads Bill Smart, Q.C. "He's the best," Alan says.

BY SOME MIRACLE of schedule juggling, that afternoon I am seated with my sister in Bill Smart's plush law office. By now the day has taken on a surreal quality. A few days ago, I would have appreciated the rich purple carpet and stylish glass coffee table, but today I note them only absently.

Beside me, Lisa squeezes my hand. Magazine pages flip in front of me; my hands are moving them, but I don't see anything except the sweeps of glossy color from what now feels like another world. The receptionist kneels to place a cup of coffee on the table. She is perfectly calm and does not spill a drop. Only rich criminals can afford this treatment, and I am not rich; I don't know how I will pay for this. A *criminal* lawyer... suddenly I am criminal. I repeat this thought over and over, trying to get it to sink into my brain.

We wait for over an hour. Finally, the office door opens, and a slight, fifty-something man projecting a powerful sense of energy welcomes me.

His questions are brief and sharp. Trying to cooperate, I answer them, but my voice is suddenly choked. Tears spill on his rich oak conference table and I can no longer speak. Like a therapist who is used to displays of emotion, he hands me a box of tissues.

Dimly, I listen to him as he begins my legal education. "In order to lay a charge, Crown counsel needs two things: First, there must be enough evidence, and second, it must be in the public's best interest to charge you. Since you admitted your relationship, now they will be looking for evidence that what you've said is true. Believe it or not, you cannot be convicted purely on your own word. If you walk in to the police station and tell them you just robbed a bank, for example, that's not enough in the way of evidence to indict you on armed robbery." He continues the seminar, and I find myself listening intently, focusing as I used to in university, learning about this foreign subject under Bill's tutelage.

"So, if the police can corroborate your story—and they'll probably try to get statements from your students, your ex-partner, the teacher you told, and anyone who might have seen you two together—the Crown will have to decide whether it's in the public's best interest to charge you. Now, everyone has the right to remain silent. So, some people may not give a statement, but some will."

Bill places his long fingers together and leans his elbows forward on the glossy table. "Given that your relationship was consensual, that Troy's mother is supportive, plus the fact that it was only actually illegal for the first five months, until Troy turned eighteen, the Crown may elect not to lay a charge."

This is the first good news I have heard in days, and I grab hold of it desperately. He tells me more things, about summary versus indictable charges, about how to read the charge in the criminal code. "You're intelligent; go do the reading," Bill says confidently.

I leave Bill's office stunned but suddenly feeling like I have a small measure of control. He has given me tasks and research to do, and I will do it. I feel an immediate sense of relief. I realize that I have not eaten all day. As I am leaving his office, Bill says, "One more thing. Anything you say to the press can be used against you in court. So do *not* talk to anyone."

MY SISTER COMES BACK to Gibsons with me. The following day I receive the next phone call that will change my life. I think I am at rock bottom, but I am wrong. It is Mark. "I just had a conversation with a reporter from the *Province,*" he says. "Standing out in my driveway. He was looking for you. I didn't tell him where you lived, but they'll probably figure it out soon."

He sounds shocked. The *Province?* Holy shit, that means this is a big story. Lisa and I pull down all the blinds and tack blankets up to the windows.

Troy's mom calls. "I've been getting calls all day from the newspapers," she says. "And this morning, I heard the story on the radio."

"That's it," Lisa says. "You've got to get out of here."

"Where?"

"I don't know, we'll go to Mom's on the first ferry and see from there."

I look around the room at my little cabin, wondering what it will feel like to see my name in the papers, to be the news.

The next morning I pack a bag, not knowing how long I will be gone. I put my two cats into their cat carriers. At the ferry, Lisa and I sit in the lineup like fugitives. It feels almost like a game; this can't possibly be real, this running and hiding. Getting off the ferry in West Vancouver, I breathe a sigh of relief. We made it. We stop at the North Vancouver Save-On-Foods, where I have been a thousand times, to grab some groceries for our encampment. As I step onto the rubber mat and the door swings open, I am confronted by the next shock.

There, in the foyer, with its racks of newspapers, is my smiling Chatelech yearbook photo, superimposed on a full-page picture of Chatelech, with the words in inch-high block letters,

"Student Sex Scandal." The entire front page of the *Province* newspaper. Me, on the cover. Scandal. Troy and I are a scandal.

Involuntarily, I step backward, horrified. This cannot be real, but it is. I imagine Mark, walking by the local Super-Valu and seeing this. I think about Troy, who never reads the paper, ripping the pages and stuffing them into his scrapbook, his friends slapping him on the back and congratulating us on our fame as a couple, not understanding the humiliation I feel. The front page. "Scandal," I repeat the word out loud, thinking of Bill Clinton and Monica Lewinsky.

"Go sit in the car," Lisa commands. "I'll just run in for a minute, I promise."

One foot, then the next. I sit in the passenger seat of Lisa's Honda, staring through the windshield. Suddenly, Lisa opens the car door and tosses the paper to me. She says, "When I was at the till, the checkout girl said, 'It's just like that Mary Kay Letourneau woman.'" The checkout clerk is referring to the elementary school teacher in the U.S. who was sent to jail for sleeping with her Grade 6 student. But Troy is eighteen!

I force myself to read the article. The words are harsh, inflammatory. They have quoted students I don't know and didn't teach. I have not been charged with anything yet, but the article says I could receive up to five years in jail for sleeping with Troy. I read the words over and over, picturing the reporter talking to my students in the Chatelech parking lot.

Lisa takes me to our mom's and we sit in the basement bedroom in North Vancouver, which is the only place I can feel safe right now. From my mother's phone I check my messages in Gibsons. "You have twenty-two new messages," the synthetic voice says. Twenty-two? There are four from students—Christine, Jill, Erin, Meghan—offering their love and support. There is one from my lawyer, Bill, reminding me not to say anything to reporters and to call him if I need him. The rest are from reporters—from the *Vancouver Sun,* from Global TV, from the *National Post* (God, that's Canada-wide)—wanting to speak to me, wanting "my side of the story." There is even a message from some radio station in the U.S., asking me to speak on their morning show.

I feel sick. My life is public property. They can say whatever they want about me, can publish people's theories and opinions, and people will read it as if it's fact because it's written down; it's in the paper. I have never seen the media this way before, never seen the elements that go into making something "news." The male teachers I know about who lost their jobs for having relationships with their students didn't generate this kind of publicity. "It's because you're a woman," Bill says over the phone. "And because, secretly, every boy wants to sleep with his teacher." What? Troy, I need to talk to you. I need to hear your calm voice, I need some sanity.

I call Troy that night, and his voice is normal. I can hear his friends in the background, yelling, "Hey, she's on the news again!" He is still comforting me, telling me it's OK. But it's not. He doesn't understand what I'm going through. In his social group he is a hero for landing his teacher, and for making the papers, although the brush with fame is primarily mine since they cannot publish his name. He doesn't understand that I feel afraid, that I can't eat, that less than two weeks since my meeting with Clifford Smith I can feel my hip bones getting sharper through my skin.

For the next two days I stay at my mom's, making lists of things I need to do, like finding out how much money I can pull out of my savings and calling my landlord to apologize for the reporters surrounding my house. My mother and her husband, Paul, are great, but I am feeling trapped in their small basement, and for the rest of the week I move in with my friend Juli.

The media add a whole new dimension to my situation, turning it from an employment issue to a full-on societal debate, complete with lights and cameras. I am used to thinking that the news happens to other people, and it astonishes me that people can voice such vehement opinions without knowing me, without knowing Troy. Before this, it has not occurred to me that real people with real lives are being followed and hounded by cameras and reporters. It is just the news, and I have always accepted it without thinking about newspapers trying to sell more copies, or TV stations trying to capture viewers.

Every error makes me angry, every insinuating sentence makes me rage against the injustice. They cannot even get our ages right, for God's sake. They keep repeating that I could serve up to five years in prison. But Bill says that would only be for a serious repeat pedophile, that ten years ago a vice-principal was charged for having sex with a fifteen-year-old student in his bathtub, and he was let go with a fine. He also tells me that these times are different.

People write to the paper about the case, some saying that Troy is eighteen now and he knew what he was doing; some calling me a sexual predator, a child molester. The moral outrage is strong; it comes through in the letters from parents, raging against me. A mother of a sixteen-year-old boy rants, "I know karate and I'm not afraid to use it." These people don't know me or Troy. But they are very angry.

I follow Juli through her daily routine for the rest of the week. Her mother is wonderful. One morning she forces me to eat breakfast and says, "It could easily have been my daughter in that situation. And your boyfriend—he's a hunk, that's for sure." From the living room that evening, Juli's dad, a stern, silent man, calls out, "Hey, that's Heather on the TV!" Juli rolls her eyes. "My dad just figured it out."

I cannot bring myself to watch the coverage, but I can hear Rebecca, one of my Math 11s, saying, "They're in love; just leave them alone," and Caitlin, in the same class as Rebecca, saying, "She was a great teacher." I hear the anchorman describe how my students threw rocks at the Global TV van as it pulled out of the Chatelech parking lot. One girl, he says, even mooned the television cameras. I feel a wave of affection for my kids, whom I haven't seen in two weeks. Oh you guys, I love you, thank you, I am so grateful for your support, I admire your guts. "Hang in there," says Erin, another student, on my answering machine. "Be strong."

In Vancouver, bigger and more anonymous, I feel safer than in Gibsons. Juli, trying to keep me going, takes me out for dinner and to a movie. Yesterday Greg Moore, the young Vancouver race car driver, was killed in a race. His face replaces mine on the front page. Although I feel sad for his family, I am grateful for the distraction.

Each day I talk to Troy on the phone. I am stressed and I need to see him. "But we can't go to my house or your mom's;

the reporters are there every day. Can you think of anywhere we can go?"

"I'll talk to Les," he says.

The next day I drive off the ferry and straight to his work. His friends are standing around their cars, waiting with him for me. "Hey," Brian says, as I step out of my car, "how's it going?"

"I've been better," I say.

"Yeah, no kidding, eh? There were reporters here at the mill looking for Troy, and one followed him through the mall yesterday." Brian shakes his head in disbelief. "Hang in there you guys."

Troy climbs into the passenger seat and we raise our hands in goodbye. Gently, as if he is scared to add to my stress, he tells me that the police came to his house at 11:30 last night and arrested him, charging him with assault for attacking Daniel back in the summer. "Oh Troy," I say sorrowfully.

We stop briefly at his mom's place to grab a change of clothes, and Troy checks the messages. Donna has moved into her parents' place for the week to rid herself of the voracious calls from the media. We are nervous here and start at any noise. Outside, dark rain is pounding, but we are hunted, fugitives, and must keep moving. Troy drives the twisting road to Pender Harbour, where Les lives. We see headlights in the rearview mirror. Is it the press? We keep driving, turning our heads away from the windows at every set of lights. There is no escape, no safety. We are not just Troy and Heather anymore, though Troy appears to be taking the media attention in stride. I am glad that he is enjoying the celebrity—or at least not hurting—but it makes me feel more alone in my humiliation. The whole drive out to Les's place we barely speak.

In Les's warm living room, we both begin to relax. After cooking dinner, we sit on his carpeted floor eating and reading the mound of papers. "I've been saving all the articles for your mother," Les says to Troy proudly. Troy and I read the more outrageous lines out loud to each other. Finally, exhausted from the tension, we escape to the bedroom in Les's basement. Faces close together for the first time in over a week, we talk quietly, wrapped up in our blankets. "Hey," Troy says softly, stroking my hair.

"Hey," I reply.

"How's it going?" he asks.

I laugh. We are not discussing, not planning, not even articulating our thoughts. I do not tell him how upset I am at his assault charge; we don't talk about my feelings about leaving my career so suddenly, or about how devastating all the media attention is for me, or how he is actually enjoying some of it. He cannot possibly know how it feels to lose the career I loved, or how much remorse wells up inside me late at night.

"Oooh, I've been better," I say. He tucks my head into his armpit as if he is about to run with a football. I lie with his warmth curled around me and feel a wave of gratitude. Our experiences are so different; we are such different people. Even through this crisis, Troy doesn't worry about what will happen to us or whether the world thinks this or that. I both envy and am disarmed by his ability to shrug things off. Yet he sees that I am in pain and is doing his best to comfort me. We are intimate strangers, our lives thrown together in a strange and artificial situation. We have gone from hiding to national fame in a two-week period. Already I can see that this crisis will either pull us together or magnify our differences dramatically. We are not a normal couple; nothing about our relationship has ever been normal. One way or another, I sense, our relationship, our lives, are about to change irreversibly. I am desperately frightened of what those changes will be.

# 16

# The Other Side

*I* AM CLEANING CAT CAGES. There is a method to this; you scrape the pungent litter into the large garbage cans and wipe up the cage while a cat sits inside it looking at you, outraged. Other cats outside the cage wind around my legs, and I juggle food and water dishes while trying to prevent these escape artists from dashing through my legs and out the door.

I have decided to volunteer at the SPCA in Gibsons. I need something, anything, to do that will distract me from the rapid and very public disintegration of my life, even if it is cleaning up cat shit.

When I walked into the SPCA two weeks ago and filled out the volunteer form, I listed my experience with my own cats as one of my qualifications. I skipped the part about previous employment entirely, and no one asked me any questions except about my experience with animals.

I love cats and have two of my own, but holding down a full-time job has meant that I have never been able to volunteer during the week. In the SPCA's cramped quarters with cages stacked to the ceiling, I meet Helen, Marie, Sandi, and Wendy. Wendy, an SPCA employee, is distinguished only by her uniform; everyone here works equally hard. Wendy shows me how to clean the room crammed with cats with maximum efficiency, how to mix the disinfectant with bleach to kill the germs, and how to use the spray bottle to discourage cat fights.

I find this work soothing; there is a regular schedule to it, and I don't have to talk to anybody. No one asks me questions, and at least I have a reason to get up in the morning. I commit to being there Wednesdays, incognito in my sweatpants and T-shirt, and I look forward to it as a place where I can do hard physical work for four hours, stopping only for raucous coffee breaks.

By now my presence in the papers has decreased to an article once every few days, so I try to act as normal as possible. If the women at the SPCA recognize my name, they don't let on. I feel welcomed and accepted as long as I learn quickly and work hard. The women here have lived difficult lives. They are hard and strong, weathering abusive boyfriends, single motherhood, some even the welfare system. All of them can name each of the thirty-plus cats easily and recall feline tenants of years gone by. I am impressed by their memories and their compassion for animals, and I feel grateful for their acceptance. They don't need to know that I am well educated, a teacher, and have a place in society that is now in jeopardy. With my hair pulled into a ponytail and rubber gloves on my hands, I keep my mouth shut so that nobody will know who I am.

I feel ashamed of the attention I have brought to the school and of the fact that other teachers will suffer because of the public's perception of my actions. I cringe to think about how all my years of teaching are now called into question, how my students and colleagues are being asked by the police about my conduct throughout my career. I want to keep feeling safe here, and I keep my head down.

"Yeah, I hope to get off welfare soon," Marie says. "But it's tough, you know, to find anything that pays more than minimum wage part-time, which, after taxes, is the same as I'd make on welfare. So I do volunteer work here because I love the animals, and hopefully one day they'll hire me."

I have never met anybody living on welfare before. I look at her and wonder what the differences between us are. I think about how I was expected my whole life to go to university and to win a full scholarship to finance those years as well. I think about all the people at SFU like me who took it for granted that they could be there, and the others, like Mark, who ate Kraft Dinner for months so that they could afford to go. I wonder if I will soon be like Marie, and the possibility shocks me. I am educated; I have lots of skills. Yes, but I can't teach anymore, I got suspended from my last job, I have no references. And who's going to hire me with my name in tatters all over the newspapers? I want to work. But some deep survival instinct kicks in, and I push my doubts aside. I will find work; I have to.

EACH DAY THAT I am not at the SPCA or in a lawyer's office, I go to the local employment center. The intake woman, Angel, seems puzzled by my presence there but diligently walks me through the center, pointing out the computers and fax machine and the job posting board with its meager offerings. Angel says, "I guess you know how to use a computer . . ." And from this I interpret that she knows who I am.

I nod. "Yes, I taught business computer applications."

"Most of our postings are for semiskilled-type work, but I'll keep my eye out for something that would suit your qualifications."

"Thank you," I say, grateful for her professionalism. I look around the room. There are a lot of men, many wearing jeans and baseball caps. The resource-based workforce in this town is in trouble. I help someone turn on a computer. Each day I spend about an hour in this room, going first to the job board and then to the computer, where I work on my resume or cover letters to be faxed in response to the low-paying secretarial jobs on offer, the only ones for which I now qualify. Between this and the SPCA, I have structure in my life. I have a place to go every day, and I hold onto my sanity.

Just before Christmas, I am interviewed by a man who owns a small business with his wife. When I explain my situation, he questions me closely about the potential charge and about how I am handling the stress of the past two months. Then he decides to give me a chance as his office manager. I cry with relief. To celebrate I go with Troy and his friends to a Vancouver Canucks hockey game. Tom's girlfriend, Cherie, gives us our only Christmas card this year, and our first one written "To Troy and Heather." It looks strange to me, and I stare at the envelope for a while. "I hope next year is better for both of you; you sure deserve it," she writes.

Like a robot, I go to work and come home each day. On the weekends, I hide and cry or make lists. There is no reason to keep our relationship a secret anymore, so Troy spends every night at my house. He does not pay rent, but he cooks and takes out the garbage on Wednesday mornings before he drives to work at the mill in Wilson Creek. I am grateful for his presence, because I am not fun to be around right now. Some primal survival instinct is overtaking me. Work, live, hide. Each day my sense of terror at being charged grows. I have taken to praying each night.

In the morning Troy tells me that he loves me. Not in a casual way, but in a full-body, life-and-death embrace, as if he is holding on for air. Gradually he fills up drawers in my house with clothes transferred from his mom's place. We make plans to spend New Year's Eve together. Sometimes I miss Mark's practical, take-charge attitude that made me feel so safe and yet so trapped, but mostly I just hang on to Troy.

I call Joanne in Quesnel, thinking that Troy and I can go and see her for a while, get away. She has known about my situation for six months, and I assume that she will be sympathetic. But when I hear the tone in her voice I know that I am mistaken. It takes her less than a minute to end our friendship forever. "When I read about it in the paper, I just couldn't handle it," she says. "I don't think you're taking responsibility for what you've done."

"Oh," is all that I can think of to say. People are falling into two camps. I am losing badly, losing my job, losing my life, losing my friends.

"I guess we'll talk later," she says. But we never do.

I will get used to this—losing friends in this manner, with many things unsaid—but right now it hurts. I think about all the colleagues I called friends at the school, how not one of them has called me, how they have simply disappeared from my life. Seeing Jenny, a colleague who lived across the street from Mark and me, in the parking lot at the IGA is sobering. When she knows that I have seen her, she says hi quickly and dives into the interior of her van to avoid further conversation. Other teachers simply pretend not to see me, or swerve quickly down a different aisle at London Drugs.

In some strange twist, many parents of kids I've taught do call me, expressing their support. Natalie, Kyle's mom, says, "I understand what you're going through." David, Adrienne's dad, asks me, "Would you still be interested in tutoring my daughter?" I get letters and cards from parents and even from people who have just read about me in the paper, expressing their support. These sparks of kindness burn small holes in the plastic wrap I am trying to keep tight around my emotions, and gratitude comes through.

I let my answering machine pick up my calls. I have only a few friends left. Dinner parties, home renovations, and Christmas cards belong to another world. Like those plants that live on air, I exist on the words Troy gives me each morning. "I love you," he says. My world has narrowed to this point.

When I get home from work on Friday nights, I feel a sense of relief. Each week is an accomplishment. It's as if I am on some giant exercise machine that only stops on the weekends. I feel skinny and exhausted.

Calling from work one evening in March, Troy asks, "What are you doing tonight? A bunch of people are hanging out at Tom's. Want to come?"

"OK," I agree, not knowing what I am getting myself into. My Friday evenings have always involved dinner parties, or a bottle of wine served with cheese and crackers, maybe a movie, hopefully some good conversation. I know that this will be different, and I feel nervous but happy that he has invited me. I can sense Troy's excitement at finally being able to be with me in his social circle, of being able to show off his now famous girlfriend to his friends. I dress for him this evening, putting on tight blue jeans and a cropped top and jean jacket. Above the waistband of my jeans, cut low in the new style, my tattoo is visible. I dress young, sure that finally I will get to see what I missed as a teenager.

Tom's parents' house is large and suburban, with white vinyl siding and enough bedrooms to accommodate three teenagers. Leading me into the basement, Troy introduces me to his group of friends, some of whom I recognize from school, some of whom I have even taught, sprawled around the room.

"Hi, Ms. Ingram," Lila says.

"Call me Heather, please." A giggle erupts from the cluster of girls at the end of the couch. They are poring over a copy of *Seventeen*. They are wearing heavy black eyeliner and tight black pants and tank tops, their barely formed breasts pushed high into padded bras. I am shocked to realize that they can't be more than fourteen. Age differences between kids don't seem to mean much in this small town, where most of them have known each other since elementary school.

I feel out of place in this room, with its bare concrete floors and worn-out couches. The kids seem as hesitant to have me here as I am to be here. I imagine that they are wondering, "Will she act like a teacher? Will she rat us out for smoking pot or drinking?" In a way it feels normal to be surrounded by teenagers, almost like my classes at the school, but it is different. We are on their turf, not mine, and I need to be the one who fits in.

Troy leaves me to my own devices and engages Tom in a fierce Ping-Pong competition. Jen, with long brown hair and large eyes, formerly in my math class and now struggling with Grade 11 in a self-paced night-school program, notices the panic on my face. She links her arm through mine and leads me to a spot on the couch. "Want a sip?" she says. She is drinking a Kahlua mudslide—a "girlie drink," as Brian informs her. "Fuck off," she says coldly, as if used to his derision.

I am grateful for Jen's leadership. I feel pressure to quickly absorb the rules and customs of the young people around me, as I know that it is important to Troy to have me be a part of his world. I calculate that I am twice as old as some of the younger girls here, and the thought makes me uneasy. I know how to talk to teenagers when the subject is math, but will we find any commonality when the purpose is strictly social? I look around me at the unlined faces, trying to find some clues as to how I should act.

Everyone is friendly and welcoming. Although I am an alien here, as the evening wears on, I feel safe for the first time in weeks. The kids seem to relax too, migrating in groups out to the garage to share a "doobie." The television is on and the stereo booms at the same time. Using my best teacher skills, I engage a young girl reading on the couch in conversation. "Anything interesting in there?" I ask.

She looks at me tentatively, as if I might call her parents at any moment. I am probably not much younger than her mom. "Oh yeah," she says. "These boots are cool, and I like this blue sweater."

We bend our heads over the page together. "Not bad," I say. "The jeans are OK too." She smiles at me.

From the corner there is a crash; kids are getting drunk, and the noise in the room is increasing. Someone has knocked a pile of CDs onto the concrete floor, and the plastic cases fly everywhere. Across the room, Troy has a beer in one hand and is spinning around like a helicopter. In another corner, Lila and Brian are engaged in a low-volume but volatile-sounding argument.

I turn back to the girl I am sitting beside and see that she is looking at Troy, his shirt flying open as he lopes around the room. She sighs. "You think he's attractive?" I ask.

She looks at me as if I am the densest person she has ever met. "Ye-ah," she says sarcastically.

All at once the door to the garage opens, and Brian charges in. There is noise, bottles are flying, Brian pushes Tom hard, their bodies falling against the coffee table. Girls scatter, Brian and Tom are punching, wrestling, their faces red. The air is ferocious. Other boys pile in, trying to pull these two off each other. They are yelling, "Fuck you, man. You're dead."

"No! Stop it!" Lila screams.

The cause of the fight is not clear but seems fueled by alcohol and a long-standing jealousy. As the violence moves randomly around the room, I am plastered against the wall in fear. Why is this happening?

Troy makes his way over to me quickly. "It's OK," he says. "They do this all the time." My breathing is quick and shallow. The boys' friends pull them apart; they are still yelling obscenities at each other. One storms out the door, slamming it deafeningly behind him. "Fuck you!" "Asshole!"

My hands are shaking. The evening has been shattered for me, but the kids fall naturally back into the space that was occupied by the fight and continue their conversations. A few cluster around Lila, Brian's girlfriend, in tears at one end of the couch. The whole drive home I think about the party. It was less fun than simply foreign to me, and I can't help thinking how unhealthy it is that all these kids smoke cigarettes, how shocked I am at the amount of pot, how conventional it seems that the girls gossip or talk clothes while the boys get drunk and fight. I know that I will soon tire of this type of party. I also know that Troy would be restless in five minutes at the type of dinner party I used to have with Mark. Yet I am used to young people from teaching and believe that I can adapt, believe that Troy and I can find a way to bridge these differences. Right now I am grateful to these teenagers for accepting me when my peers have not.

The next day but a universe away, Vanessa, Bill's assistant, calls me at work. Her young, fresh voice fills my ear. "Is it OK to fax you over some papers?" she asks, her voice indicating nothing unusual.

Although Bill has warned me that this day is coming, I'm unprepared for it, and my stomach seizes. I print out page upon page of legal language, the whole thing, my charge of a single count of Sexual Exploitation, the statements, everything. Vivian is in there, giving her version of the story and leaving out all the parts where she was supportive of me. Clifford Smith is in there, going to the police to report that I smiled when I was given my letter of suspension, interpreting my stress to imply that I was proud of it. Bruce Jansen's handwritten notes to himself about our conversation are in there. So is Mark, who has also spoken to the police, telling them that he thinks I am not a bad person but that I should be forced to work in a shelter for disadvantaged women.

Seeing it all is shocking, like suddenly being able to read the minds of all the people around me. I feel betrayed, hurt, and angry, yet I also understand why Vivian, Clifford, and Mark have said what they did. I picture Mark spending hours in front of his computer, drafting a statement for the police about me. There are things missing too. Although I know from the papers that the police have been trying to get my students to give statements, not one student has spoken to the police. Having seen Troy pursue me so openly for months, most of them know his side of it. As one girl said on the news, as long as I continued to run my classroom in a professional and equitable manner, what we did outside of class time was our business. Now, five months after my suspension in October, the charge is official. The newspaper stories intensify again.

One rare night, Troy and I go for a drive into Sechelt. Although our relationship is now legal, I am so afraid of being in public, of seeing ex-colleagues, and of generating more media attention that I stay home most of the time I am not at work. Tonight, Troy is filling his car with gas at the only gas station in town open past eight o'clock. Across the street, a group of teenagers waves to me. I get out of the car and walk over to see them. "Hi, Ms. Ingram!" My ex-students hug me.

"We miss you so much! The new accounting teacher is horrible!" Rita says.

I sit down on the bench amid a flurry of kids, telling me their lives all at once. "I'm doing so great in my math," Keith says.

"I got a grad dress!" Caitlin says. I am as excited to see them as they are to see me.

When the initial flurry is over, a small silence ensues. Then Sean, one of my alternate kids, looks at me and says bluntly, "You screwed up, Ms. Ingram."

I feel Sean's words settle in as the truth. There is no possibility of denial. By my actions I have damaged not only myself but each one of my students, who believed in me and benefited from my teaching. For the first time I see things from their perspective and feel the enormity of my selfishness. Because of me, they lost a good teacher. It's simple and tragic. I cannot do anything but accept this, feel this reality. I look at Sean and say, "I know. I'm sorry."

IT IS AN APRIL SUNDAY, the day before I must be in court. No more running from the media; they will be unavoidable, and, I fear, out in full force. The day is almost hot; summer is in the air. I could spend the day inside, or I could go out and try to fight my fear of what will happen tomorrow. At Juli's urging, we go with Troy and his friends to the Sechelt drag races, spreading blankets on the grass and rolling up our sleeves to get some sun on our winter-white arms. About five thousand people, well over half the population of Sechelt, are spread out on the large airstrip field.

Al, the husband of one of my ex-colleagues, walks by me. "Hi, Heather," he smiles. Troy and I are sitting shoulder to shoulder, and I smile back, surprised and thrilled that he has acknowledged me. A normal day, God, I feel like a normal person today. The loudspeaker in the distance announces the next cars to race, and I feel lighter than I have in months.

Late that night, around 10:30 P.M., Troy and I are asleep. The next day will be brutal, we know, and we are in bed early in preparation. I wake to a sharp knock on the door. When I open it, a police officer, Constable Rosenberg, is standing there. What? I've already been charged, doesn't he know I have a court date tomorrow? "Is Troy Robertson here?" the officer asks.

In a daze, I wake Troy up. "Troy, it's the police for you." Wrapping my bathrobe around him, Troy goes to the door. I cannot hear their brief conversation. The door closes.

"What's going on?" I ask. I can't believe this.

He says, "I'm being charged with sexual assault."

"What???"

He takes a deep breath. "I picked up a hitchhiker. We fooled around a bit in the car and then the cops pulled up. It was nothing."

"How old was she?" I ask.

"I thought she was, like, sixteen, but it turns out she was thirteen."

"When did this happen?"

"Back in October."

I fall back on the bed, unable to process this information. "Why?"

"To get back at you for your thing in the summer," he says. "I'm sorry."

I am speechless. This happened almost six months ago, sometime around my birthday, just before I lost my job. I am astonished that he didn't tell me. I feel hurt and betrayed. We need to talk about this, alone and unhurried, but there are too many other things to worry about right now.

The next day, we are up early, putting on nice clothes, walking around each other, not discussing the policeman at the door last night. My sister is here, and with her support I hold it together. The news of Troy's charge has already been spread to the newspapers, and I struggle to think who could have called them, since he was only served his papers last night. My dad calls me to ask about it. I can only say, "I don't know." I feel as if I have stepped into a surrealist painting, where the elements look real but nothing makes sense. God is lobbing water balloons at me. Ha! You think you're coping? OK, deal with *this!* Troy and I are accumulating an enormous amount of emotional baggage. This morning, for the public, we will be strong. This afternoon, I tell myself, I can fall apart.

Later in the week, after I have entered my guilty plea, after the media insanity has subsided a bit, I read the police report of Troy's charge. He and a young girl, parking in a car by the side of the road. The officer recognizing Troy's car and stopping to investigate. Her shirt up, his pants unbuttoned. He has not asked how old she is. The police ask Troy to come in and make a statement, which he does, on videotape, with no lawyer, saying that they did not have intercourse and that their contact was consensual. The officer is relentless in his questions, probing, graphic, harsh. He tries to get Troy to say more. The police call the girl's mother, who does not indicate that she wants to press charges. Her daughter has been involved with older men before, she says, and she is worried about her. Nothing happens for almost six months. Troy believes that the problem has been handled. He tells me nothing. Then, three days before the charge is due to expire under the statute of limitations, a charge is laid, at my home, the night before my court date. And the news is in the papers before we even know about it. I shake; I can't stop shaking.

Every faith I have is now gone. Fairness, justice, the law, the police . . . These institutions are meaningless to me. My trust in Troy has foundered. I feel betrayed, but more than that . . . I feel as if I have crossed an invisible barrier that I can only refer to as "the other side." I see things I did not see before. There is nothing of my old life left. I am subhuman now, beyond caring about anything. My hair stays in a ponytail. I pull away from Troy when he tries to touch me. The newspapers rage on about me. I pull my curtains closed and lock my door. Lying on my couch, my arms wrapped around myself, I stare at the ceiling. I feel numb. Although I am not eating, my stomach feels full all the time. I don't even cry anymore.

# { 17 }

# *Isolation*

*T*HE MONTH FOLLOWING my first court date goes by quickly, and soon I am back again, on Monday, May 29, 2000. When I leave work the previous Friday with a pile of paper in my in-basket, I say to my boss, "I hope I'll be able to come to work on Tuesday morning."

"I have faith that you will," she says confidently. My employers have been so supportive.

Déjà vu. I am standing in front of the same judge, with the same contingent of supporters on the left, but now even more media on the right side of the courtroom. Crown counsel talks for over an hour, listing case after case of older male teachers who seduced young female students, describing their exploits in excruciating detail. I feel physically sick listening to the descriptions of how they seduced these young girls. But I am being charged with the same crime, being compared to these men. Some of the men are in jail, whereas others have merely been fined; there seems to be little consistency except that as more charges are laid against teachers over the years the penalties get stiffer.

My lawyer speaks for about fifteen minutes, noting that I have an excellent teaching record and no previous criminal record, and that both Troy and his mother are fully behind me. He says that this is the only case he has seen in which the victim refused to give a victim impact statement to the police and asks the judge for a suspended sentence. Crown counsel asks for eight months incarceration. The judge, calling my behavior an affront to society, overrides both requests and gives me ten months of strict house arrest, with one hundred hours of community service and a year's probation to follow. I imagine my parents sitting at home, waiting for me to call them, maybe wondering where they went wrong, certainly never wanting this for their elder daughter. I wonder how they will cope with this news.

I wipe my tears, and bracing ourselves, Troy and I leave the court and walk down the long steps to the landing. It is like walking into a swarm of blackflies. The buzzing and clicking begin as soon as we hit the steps and intensify with each step down. Ten fat microphones are pressed within inches of our mouths. Dozens of cameras flash lights in our eyes. With Troy squeezing my hand, I say something about having learned a lot from this experience. I just want to go home.

Although we are prepared for the media this time, their presence is still horrible and disruptive. Three times that day I see Donna driving back and forth on the highway, running from the seemingly endless stream of reporters. In Sechelt, Brian's girlfriend, Lila, waves me down, and we chat briefly.

"You're all over the news, you know. The TV cameras were up at the school again, interviewing all your students."

"I know, they came to my house; that's why I'm driving around."

She hugs me. "Take care of yourself. See you soon."

Troy automatically screens my calls. I can't even read the media stories anymore, and the debate rages on without me about what our schools are coming to and what an immoral person I am. But now that our relationship has lasted almost two years, the reporters are trying to get "the other side of the story." The *Province* reporter on the phone, the one who wrote the most damaging and insinuating stories, spends almost fifteen minutes trying to convince me to give an interview. "I've changed my mind about you," he says, and my last assumptions about the impartiality of the media fall away. Did I really believe before this experience that the newspapers just report the news?

I am required to report to my "supervisor," Sue Davies, within seventy-two hours for my house arrest—the "real" punishment—to begin. For ten months, I will only be allowed to leave my home to go to work and, one hour a week, to go to the local mall for groceries and banking. Although my sentencing documents have already been read aloud to me by the court registrar, the rules state that Sue must read each word of them to me again. I sit in front of Sue, a criminology major about my age, my emotions raging and raw but my face impassive. She picks up the phone and schedules the psychological evaluation, which is mandatory for all sex offenders. Then Troy and I drive home, where I will spend the next ten months of my life.

That night, the first of my incarceration, I cry so hard that Troy looks scared. "Please stop," he begs me. Even after he falls asleep, exhausted himself from the last few long, public, and emotional days, tears continue to leak from my eyes, and my stomach muscles constrict.

THE BUILDING MUST HAVE been decorated in the seventies, and by now it is well worn. I think, I am a criminal now; to society I am not worth any more than this. In the psychologist's office, I sit at a large polished table. He sits beside me, with a clipboard and lots of papers, and asks me about Troy, our relationship, how it began, how I feel about him. I tell the man the truth. In response to his questions, I describe how we feel about each other, how he teaches me things, how we are struggling right now to reach a peace with each other despite the barrage of events around us.

As I speak I watch the psychologist's face. Have I really learned nothing from this experience? Do I not yet understand that honesty is rarely the best policy? Can I not now describe to someone in graphic language that what I learned in school and in the "real world" are very different? The sitcoms and the news are equally fantasy. What is the point of this? We have been talking for about forty-five minutes, and now it is time for me to fill out the multiple-choice "test." Along with the doctor's interview, it is supposed to determine how much of a danger I am to society.

The test questions are transparent, designed for male rapists and pedophiles, and I wonder as I am filling in circles on the electronic scan sheet whether any real psycho would not be able to lie his way through this test without blinking. From my teaching experience I recognize that the questions are designed to test for roughly five standard psychological anomalies, including obsessive-compulsive disorder, eating disorders, and delusions. One question asks whether I believe that "women in short skirts are asking to be raped" (No!), and others whether I generally put work before play (Yes). Have I been on the cover of more than two national magazines in the past year? I know the question is designed to test for delusions, so I circle No, thinking of the *Elm Street* cover that carried my photo a few weeks before. The line between sanity and insanity is very thin, I think.

The psychologist thanks me and then writes his report, which will say that because I claim that Troy initiated our relationship, I am not taking sufficient responsibility for my crime. I am refused a copy of this report, so I file a Freedom of Information request through the provincial government to get a copy. I wonder how people who can't even read well enough to fill out a form fare in this system.

My supervisor says that the psychologist's report has determined that I am not a danger to society. That means, she says, that there is no counseling available to me—only high-risk sex offenders qualify. The one benefit that might be gained from this experience is not possible.

My mother and Paul call me once a week and take the ferry from North Vancouver as often as Paul's work schedule allows, bringing me groceries and supplies, running out to buy oil for my car or weather stripping for my door. I fear that the stress of my situation will push my mom into another depressive phase, but she seems to be holding it together. They invite Troy and me to come for dinner many months from now, when I will be able to leave my house.

My dad makes the one-hour drive down from Pender Harbour to visit me every few weeks. When I talk about Troy he is silent; our conversation is about my work, my sister, or other safe topics. I sense that he blames Troy for my downfall, and with an instinctive mistrust of authority figures, Troy avoids being home when my parents come over.

I know my parents love me, but I am still desperate, close to insanity. With leaving Mark and losing my job, I have no friends on the Sunshine Coast. Many evenings I just sit at the computer and write. There is a hint of danger to recording my thoughts, a sense of schoolgirl defiance. They can put me under house arrest, but they can't make me stop thinking.

WORDS LIKE "sex offender" and "criminal" haunt my sleep. A probation officer. Psychiatric assessment for sex offenders. Danger to society. It is crucial that I play this game, and know the rules well, so that I can follow them exactly. This is not like regular jail, where someone is watching me twenty-four hours a day. I remember from my psychology course in university that infrequent reinforcement is more effective in creating the desired behavior than constant surveillance. If you want a kid to study consistently instead of cramming for a test, give irregular surprise quizzes.

My surprise quizzes come in the frightening form of the police. My sentence says that I am allowed to buy groceries on Wednesdays between 4:30 and 5:30 P.M., at SuperValu only. I can leave my property for no other reason besides work. If I run out of bread or milk, I have to ask someone to buy it for me. I can't go to the library. I can't go for a walk. I become convinced I will go crazy from lack of exercise, until the parent of a student at Chatelech lends me her rowing machine. But I can still make love with Troy, another ridiculous systemic contradiction.

One morning in June at the SPCA, where I am serving my community hours, I call Troy, still asleep at home. "I think you should come up here," I say. For months he has been trying to convince me that we should adopt a dog.

He is awake, immediately alert. "Why? Did you find a puppy?"

"Just come," I answer, with a smile in my voice. He hangs up, and I can picture him throwing back the red checked comforter and reaching for his jeans.

In the small enclosure where the puppies are kept, there is only one. He is brown with tigerish black stripes through his soft fur, and he has large droopy puppy ears. Everything about him is cute. I have never dealt with a puppy before, and I now have three cats, but this little guy is so friendly, so eager, that it doesn't take much for Troy and me to fall in love with him. And God, do I ever need this love in my life right now.

Together in the cage, I say, "If we break up, he's your responsibility. You need to help pay for his food and take him for walks. Remember, I'm under house arrest; I can't even walk him."

"I know, I know," Troy says.

And with that we become dog parents. Troy names him Seymour, which reminds me of a character in J.D. Salinger's books. A literary reference, and besides, as he tears around my living room until the cats hiss and scratch, he really looks like a Seymour. My sister is delighted that I have come to my senses and entered the world of dogs. She comes to visit with an armload of how-to books about training puppies. In the backyard, Troy runs Seymour from one end to the other, growling at him to show him no, praising him when he sits or stays.

In the evenings, Troy and I do not talk much but attempt to join our two worlds through video. We watch, with success, *Crazy in Alabama, The People vs. Larry Flynt,* and *Saving Private Ryan.* Sometimes we rent what he calls "chick movies," and he only falls asleep at the very end of *The English Patient.* When Lazlo de Almasy buys Katharine a thimble of saffron, I swoon. I try to explain my reaction to Troy, to convey the rarity of the spice, the history and romance implied by this exotic gift, and the significance of Katharine's confession at the end of the movie that she wears it throughout her marriage to another man and to her lonely death. I finger the necklace he gave me on Valentine's Day, remembering our innocence, feeling how long ago it was that we sat in the car looking at the view over the ocean.

When Troy leaves to go work on the fish boat this year, I am anxious. I cannot get my car fixed or go buy dog food. Troy has done these things for me since May, but for the next two months I will be on my own. Neither of us wants him to go. The pain of separation is intense this time. From a pay phone, he says, "I miss you so much. I just realize that you're the one I want to be with." I drink in his words. I feel this way too; everything is worth it if I get to keep this sweetness in my life. As I sit in bed with the covers wrapped around me, we croon gentle words to each other. We talk about the future, about when he gets home, and about how life will be so good for both of us. I put all my faith into his words; I am floating on them, deriving the nutrients I need for survival.

One day in August, I am walking dogs at the SPCA. I spend a lot of time volunteering because it is the only social contact I have and the only way I can give Seymour any exercise. I feel so incredibly alone, but Hanne, Sandi, Elizabet,

and Tim, all SPCA employees, smile and laugh with me as we
mop and sweep. I look at the cars driving by and wonder
what it feels like to be able to go somewhere that the police
don't know about, what it feels like to be able to get in your
car and drive somewhere without getting someone's approval
for it first.

A truck drives by and then suddenly brakes and backs up
the street. Damn, I think, a reporter. I look a mess, smell like
cats and bleach, have no makeup on. But no, it is Norm, the
chemistry teacher at Chatelech—who with his education
could be teaching at a university, but chose to inspire high
school students instead. He gets out of his truck. "Heather?"
he says gently. Norm was always so gentle. I don't know how
to speak or what I would say even if I could get words to come
forth. "I just wanted to tell you that I wish you all the best,"
Norm says. "I know that you've been though an awful lot."
His voice is kind and full of compassion.

"You're the only teacher who's said anything to me," I choke
out and then begin shaking as tears pour down. Norm watches
me, radiating gentleness, acceptance, respect. I drink it all
down; I am so thirsty. His generosity in coming back to speak
to me is overwhelming. "Thank you," I manage to get out.

Whenever he gets in to port in Prince Rupert, Troy calls
me. "I met a man who looked worse than the English patient," he says over the phone from Prince Rupert. He describes the man, burned, with no ears or eyebrows left and
only part of a nose. "It really makes you see life from a whole
new perspective, you know? How much courage it takes to
have a good life. If he can do it, I can."

I am amazed at his introspection and by his reference to
one of my movies. While Les drinks scotch at the Crest Hotel,

Troy leans in the doorway of a phone booth and talks to me long distance for hours at a time.

We agree that life and love are precious. Daily, he reminds me that all the events of the past ten months—the stress, the media frenzy, the appearance in court, the loss of my career—are minor as long as we have each other. "I'll do anything to make you happy," he says. "I even wrote you a letter, I poured my heart out into it."

When the letter arrives, ten pages filled with poems and stories, I overlook the bad spelling and feed on his words, take them into my lonely, crumbling soul. I feel so amazed and privileged to be receiving the only letter he has ever written to anyone outside of the requisite thank-you notes to his grandparents. "I love you so much," he says.

"I love you too, Troy," I say, tears spilling down.

That night I dream. In my dream Troy is an angel. He is sent to me so that I can see all the things about the world I have never seen before, good and bad, ugly and beautiful. He is sent to open me up to life, to ensure that I can never again be swamped and trapped by perfectionism or by thinking that achievement or a beautiful home can equal happiness. Death is just around the corner, he whispers, but not morbidly. In my dream this statement sounds like an invitation, just as when years ago Mark dragged me out the door in my socks to take me for a drive. Come with me, come experience, come live. Don't wait—it could be gone before you know it.

My dream fades to consciousness. I awake knowing that there is a reason for all of this. I know—though I will probably forget and have to be reminded in the future—that I am walking a path that will take me places I have never been. Lying in my bed, I feel the resurgence of something long lost,

long buried, something that slipped away so quietly that I
didn't notice it. Hope, maybe? I don't know. I notice the
sounds of leaves, the smell of the raccoons that prowled my
backyard last night. I savor the feeling. It feels good. It feels
as if Troy and I are going to make it. Despite everything, I
might actually be OK.

ALL THROUGH AUGUST I walk to work with Seymour, who
is growing at an astonishing rate. Without Troy around, I am
reaching the extremities of loneliness. My bosses are away on
vacation, so I spend each day in the office by myself, then each
evening at home by myself. I feel like I am living at a high al-
titude, where oxygen is rare and breathing is difficult.

My new dentist says, "You look familiar. I can't place it, but
I recognize your face." I shrug, and notice the dental assistant
shooting looks of warning at him that he can't quite interpret.

At the grocery store checkout during the one hour a week
I am permitted out to grocery shop, the clerk says casually,
"Are you going to see the opening of the new theatre?"

"No, I don't think so," I reply ambiguously, not admitting
the truth, that I *can't*.

The woman who runs the printing company from which I
order business cards for work says to me over the phone, "People should just learn to mind their own business. There's a lot
more dirty laundry in this town than anything you've done."
This I interpret to mean that she knows who I am and is offering me support. Rattled, but grateful, I thank her.

Back in May, when my house arrest started, different police officers frequently came to my house after work or in the
evenings—three times in the first week. Now, three months

later, having found me at home on each check, the visits have abated. Tonight I am sitting in my living room reading *Long Walk to Freedom,* Nelson Mandela's account of his struggle against apartheid and the years of his life spent in prison. Around 9:00 P.M. there is a knock on my door, and the usual shot of adrenaline pumps through my veins. It is a police officer. I still can't get used to it; I always feel as if they are here to tell me somebody I love has died. This officer is young, maybe twenty-five, with dark hair shaved at the sides and plump, childlike cheeks that contrast with his uniform. I recognize him as the officer who took my fingerprints before my sentencing. He told me then that he was newly graduated from his training program and had just moved his family to the Sunshine Coast. He looked embarrassed and apologized profusely when twice he mixed up which finger he was on during the inky process.

Finding me where I should be, he is friendly, and I release Seymour from my grasp on his collar. They tussle playfully in my carport. "What kind of dog is he?" the officer asks. "Does he have any pit bull in him?"

"No, no, Seymour's an SPCA mix—half Rhodesian Ridgeback, some Irish wolfhound, and probably something else," I say.

"He's a nice dog," he says kindly.

I smile. The scene is bizarre, and yet normal. I can imagine seeing this officer at the grocery store and saying hi. My fear of police and courts is at odds with this gentle man in my carport. Before the events of the past year, I have always thought of the police as the good guys, the ones you could call on when your car or your house was vandalized, the ones who, at worst, give you a well-deserved speeding ticket.

Since October, since I read Constable Rosenberg's graphic and relentless interrogation of Troy, since I have become the subject of thick stacks of paper crammed with statements from my former colleagues and evidence of my every action, my attitude has undergone a radical change; now I am afraid. I did not imagine that I could be afraid of the police in Canada. What about people in places like Afghanistan or Guatemala? How do they sleep or feel safe?

Troy calls to let me know that he has bought a motorcycle and is beginning the long drive home from Prince Rupert tomorrow. Two days later, he is on my front step, leaning against the door frame, looking tired but healthy. His hair is blonder than I have ever seen it before, there is stubble on his chin, and he has an air of experience that was not there when he left. It feels like it's been months, but it has only been six weeks. Dressed in black motorcycle gear with a helmet under his arm, he has a fresh sweatiness that makes me think of sudden rain bouncing on the hot dry wood of my back deck. When we hug I feel how right this is, how I have been craving this all my life. He has been trying to quit smoking, he says, knowing that this will please me. I am pleased. I am so grateful to have him home, and so willing to let him fill my space. I bring him inside and inhale him.

But of course it can't last. I am at work during the day and at home each afternoon at exactly 4:30. As the days shorten and the darkness begins, a restlessness invades me like cancer. Troy is back, but since his summer away, he's spending more and more time in Sechelt with his new motorcycle and his friends, away from me. I feel trapped and almost more alone than I did while he was gone. Resentful of his freedom and jealous of the people with him, I feel angry each night when he comes home. He has quit smoking, but that is not enough for me. He doesn't need the money, but I have pushed him to get his job back at the mill right away. I am controlling, but so out of control.

I read books about improving your life, planning your career change. Intent on making use of this time under house arrest, I make long lists of goals and detailed schedules for achieving them. I shove my feelings aside or express them late at night. Each night I listen for Troy's wheels to crunch in the gravel of my driveway. "Where have you been?" I ask, trying to keep the hurt and anger out of my voice. My whole soul aches.

"Just out with the boys," he says. "I'll stay in tomorrow night."

I nod. Promises are in the future, and all I have is day after day of present tense. I long to talk about this with him, to break through the barrier that is growing between us, but when I do he says that everything is all right and asks why I am getting on his case. I long to release all the feelings that are building inside me, but I am scared and I want to believe that the words we spoke during the summer can come true. If I push too much I might lose him, and then I will truly have nothing. My world is my house and whatever Troy brings into it. Increasingly, he fails to bring himself.

ON MY BIRTHDAY, October 14, Troy arrives with videos and flowers. "I've never bought flowers for anyone before," he tells me. They are beautiful.

I am sick of staying home, but we can't go out, so we curl up on the couch. Late into the second flick, just before midnight, which marks the end of my birthday, he says, "Do you want your present now?" He gets up and disappears into the bedroom.

I am mystified. Since the summer he has been trying hard to be the kind of boyfriend he sees that I want, but we still aren't talking enough. He is back to working at the mill, a job he hates. And I fiercely resent my enforced dependency on him. It is yet another ridiculous contradiction that my house arrest is putting pressure on the person who is supposed to be my victim.

Troy comes back with a small package. Inside, a plain gold band. A ring, Troy has bought me a ring for my birthday. What does this mean? I need to know what this means to him.

"Will you marry me?" he says.

There is a half-heartedness in his words that I try hard to ignore. I am excited, happy—that's what you're supposed to feel when you hear those words—but I can't ignore the sense that he is doing this solely for my benefit. I have told him I want him to grow up; is this how he is trying to do it? He is only nineteen.

"Yes," I say, and give the ring back to him to slip on my finger. It fits perfectly. We are engaged—or at least I think we are. He is so young. I remember the reporters back at my court appearance getting excited when they heard rumors that we were engaged.

But I am disappointed. This is not how I wanted this to happen, and it is not Troy's fault. I am trapped, and more than that, I am subhuman, not worthy, an ugly, angry, horrible human being, hugely resentful of the factors that have brought me to this point, including my own stupidity. I do not feel the way I am supposed to feel on the day I get engaged. It is a sad sham. Here I am under house arrest for having had a relationship five months too soon with the sweet young man who just asked me to marry him. And I don't believe he really wants to get married, or at least not yet. But he is trying to give me something, a commitment, maybe, or a reason to find hope. My heart breaks at the sweetness of this gesture, and I try to push my negative thoughts away.

# 18

# Hitting Bottom

BY NOVEMBER, Troy and I are fighting more and more. I am angry when he goes out and act suspicious when he stays in. Since the incident with the young girl in his car, I haven't trusted him to tell me everything. I lash out at him: "Why don't you get a better job? How come you're always out with your friends?" I complain about anything I can think of.

"I'll stay home more," he promises. "I'm sorry that I'm not a good boyfriend."

I spend so much time alone that I live more and more inside my own head. I grab on to thoughts and run wild with them. Anger and sadness follow me doggedly. I want to throw myself at Troy and scream, "Why are you still with me? How can you be so good, so kind to me?" Tears well up, and a lump of gratitude surfaces in my throat.

I shout to myself as I drive to work. When I hear the word "court" on the radio, I feel a sharp pang in my chest. I see evil in every police car and talk back to the radio whenever a story about injustice or corruption is broadcast. I can't watch TV or read the papers without feeling rage—rage at the huge inconsistencies in the criminal justice system, at having left the world of respectability and crossed into another place where different rules apply. I follow the story of Allen Richardson, the man who, in his fifties, after a long and respectable career in university research, is jailed for selling twenty dollars' worth of LSD in 1971. With his wife carrying cancer, he must leave his job and his life thirty years later to serve out his sentence. This is justice? The man is a pillar of society! What good does his punishment serve? Our release dates are approximately the same, and in my mind there is a kinship between us. I also rage at myself for allowing Troy to have so much power over me, and for letting love dictate my choices.

And fear. I feel so much fear each day. I lie in the bathtub, tense, listening for a police car coming to my house to check up on me. I worry that I won't be able to answer the door fast enough. I am conscious of every action, in case I have to abandon it suddenly to verify my presence at home. I am afraid of never being considered a responsible citizen again, of being tainted for life. I am afraid of adding more casualties to the list of friends I have hurt by taking my life apart. During my hour of grocery shopping time, I keep my head down as I walk through the aisles, speaking to no one, radar on high alert for anyone who might recognize me. I feel tense, frightened, and long for the safe seclusion of my house.

Occasionally I see a former colleague, who ignores me. I want to bury myself deep.

A small opportunity to still feel useful seems monumental. Wendy and Christine, former students, drop by to check on me.

"Life sucks," Christine says. "I'm fighting with my mom, and Jackie's dating the guy I like."

"I'm only allowed to have the car one night a week," Wendy says.

They describe their experiments with drugs and alcohol and sex. Their voices sound light, but I hear pain behind their words. They look sad, and suddenly I see that they are not here just because they feel sorry for me but also because they need empathy, guidance, someone to listen. Even under house arrest and no longer able to teach, I still have something to offer these girls. I grasp at the chance to feel like a whole person again and offer suggestions, murmur acknowledgment—yes, life is hard, choices are difficult, seemingly small events can have a huge impact. Given the mess my life is in, I feel unqualified to help these girls, but they don't seem to care and hug me as they leave. For a few hours, I feel valuable. The sense of healing is palpable.

Troy calls me at work one day to say that he has had a fight with his boss and has walked away from his job at the mill. I dimly detect that he is close to his limit, but I don't say anything. He is away so much now. I have the same sinking sensation I had at this time last year. Each day it is an effort to get out of bed, to speak and smile. I feel that I am always on the verge of losing consciousness.

In November, we hear that Brian's mom has died—a nightmare of alcohol and prescription medication, ending in heart failure. "Can you come to the funeral?" Lila asks.

"I don't know if I can get permission, but I will try," I promise.

My supervisor faxes me a letter of permission; I can be at the church from 1:00 P.M. until 3:00 P.M. In the church reception room, balancing tea and cake, I feel strange to be around so many people, to be part of a group again, even a sad one. As mourners leave after the service to gather for more coffee and memories, I ask Troy to drive me home.

"Another one of those sad days," he says, pulling the car into my driveway at 2:55 P.M. I nod, and as he backs away to rejoin Brian and his friends, I sit on the floor of my living room, alone, lonely, too numb to cry.

HE IS OUT all night again. I don't know where he is. I page him the next day, Thursday afternoon, December 28. When he calls me back his voice sounds far away. "What's wrong?" I ask.

"I'm just so *stressed,*" he says faintly.

Around six he arrives home. When I get to the door, he just looks at me. "I don't think we're going to make it."

My heart stops. I can't believe these words. Once he is inside, I see that he has made an irrevocable decision. He says, "I can't just be myself around you. I can never live up to your standards. I don't even know who I am anymore."

I understand; I spoke the same words to Mark two years ago. I hate that I have made him feel the same way I felt back then. I cry loudly, in outrage. "Please, Troy, please stay."

"This is the hardest thing I've ever had to do," he says. "I just don't have faith anymore that we will be together."

We lie on the bed in what has been our bedroom for almost two years, tears pouring down our faces. We are hanging on to each other. He won't get up and go; he just keeps holding on to me. I want him to keep hanging on, to say that there is still a chance, because it's obvious that we love each other, it's obvious that we are both struggling and trying and feeling like failures, but I can't prolong the pain. I get up from the bed and start throwing his clothes from the dresser into a gym bag, stuffing them in. Methodically, maniacally, I pack his things while he sits on the bed and watches me, and I almost run them out to the car, my car. I am lending him my car to leave me.

I pack dog food, because Seymour will go with him. Now I have lost everything I love. The image of them leaving will haunt me, will burn my brain and make me scratch myself to bleeding, will scrape me raw from the inside: Troy, in my car, with all of his things packed in around him, backing out of the driveway, and Seymour, sitting up in the passenger seat beside him, looking through the window at me.

Almost immediately my phone rings. It is Donna. He must have called her as soon as he left, and she, being the most incredible victim's mother a girl could ask for, is calling me to make sure that I am OK. Tomorrow morning, Donna promises, she will drive down and sit with me, talk with me, let me cry. The whole night I cry anyway, sleeping on the couch in the living room because I don't want to be in the bed Troy and I shared.

When I call Juli I can only whisper into the phone, "He left me."

"Oh no," she says. "I was praying this wouldn't happen while you were still incarcerated. I knew this fall would be the hardest time for both of you."

Friday evening Juli arrives with a bottle of Bailey's. She forces me to eat a bowl of noodles, the most I have eaten in two days. We lie in our sleeping bags on the floor. She wraps herself around me and cries with me through most of the night.

I used to be loved and accepted; I used to be mostly positive and able to cope with things—except Mark of course—but now my life is a mess. I have lost so many people. Troy is the one I thought I would get to keep forever. Why couldn't I relax and be happy and appreciate what I had with him? I wish we could rewind ourselves back to September. He wanted to improve his life, but I pushed him too hard, did not give him enough credit for the changes he did make, and so he felt it necessary to hide things from me. I miss him; I miss his phone calls and his love.

I have grieved so much over the past two years, and yet I still have more grieving to do. Perhaps I am grieving for Mark too, since I went directly from him to Troy with no time in between; I know I am still grieving the loss of my students and my career. If I survive this, I will be able to survive anything. Let him go, Heather, just let him go. Let go of the control, which is a stupid and dangerous illusion anyway. Let go of the pain, let go of the love you have for him. Trust that you will come through this OK, maybe even happy. Maybe you'll have a life one day. Troy is gone, and you can't change that, so accept it and let him go. If your love for him is real, then you know you have to let him go.

"Troy, I love you. Please come back to me," I whisper to my reflection in the darkened window.

. . .

I GO TO THE SPCA to find some degree of normalcy in cleaning up after the cats. I miss Seymour so much, and it is hard to be around dogs at all. That afternoon, New Year's Eve, Troy calls and leaves a message, "Happy New Year. I love you."

I am prepared to curl up on the couch in front of a movie for the night, but later in the evening, Lila brings a bunch of her friends to my house to keep me company. For the first time in days I feel light, and I twirl around my living room in Lila's long fake fur coat. Gerry tells me that Troy is seeing someone, a fifteen-year-old girl named Stephanie, and that he is dealing pot to earn money.

We play cards for a while, until I hear the phone ring. Sitting on the edge of my bathtub with the receiver in my ear, I strain to hear Troy's voice over the party in the background. He sounds so broken, so upset. "I just need some space and time," he says. "Every girl I've loved has ended up hurting me."

"Even me," I whisper. "Troy, I'm sorry." My heart is in little pieces on the cold vinyl floor.

There is a part of me that knows he is courageous for leaving when he was not happy, when his sense of self was fading. I did not have the courage to leave when I felt it happening with Mark so long ago. I guess I failed at being what Troy wanted me to be as well, though he is much better at just accepting who I am than I am at accepting who he is. He tried so hard to be what I wanted him to be that he ended up being afraid to be himself. Why didn't I let him make his own choices and take responsibility for them?

I try to talk rationally to myself: *Heather, your sentence will soon be over, and as dark and hard as all these days have been, spring is coming and with it will come light and laughter and perhaps even a tiny bit of joy. You have come out of this relationship with your*

*sense of self intact, your sexuality fulfilled, your beauty and intelli-*
*gence strong. Your emotions and dependencies and fears are what you*
*need to work on, and you need to find work that is fulfilling and joy-*
*ful. You have your garden, your cats, your house. Try to feel safe and*
*be a good friend to everyone who comes your way. One day you will*
*swim in the ocean and sleep under the stars.*

EACH DAY I GET up and go to work. I have become an expert
at survival. I put food into my mouth, chewing and swallow-
ing. Troy phones me about once a week, and we spend long
minutes silent on the telephone, both of us hurting through
the lines. He has moved with his fifteen-year-old girlfriend
and a crack-addicted single mother into an apartment above
the pawn shop in downtown Sechelt. "I love you," he says. "I
just need to be free. I'm not ready to settle down."

"I love you too," I say. I do.

He will not let me see his place; he calls it the shit shack.
"You won't like it. Besides, the police show up all the time."

I tell him that I'm taking custody of Seymour. He doesn't
fight me; he has other priorities now. Home again, Seymour
shoves his broad, smooth head gently into my neck and his cool,
wet tongue swipes suddenly at my face. At least I have this.

I feel a complex mixture of anger, hurt, and desire for
Troy. These feelings cloud our every interaction. "She means
nothing to me," he says of the girl he is living with. At some
level I understand that his feelings for me are in conflict with
the rest of his lifestyle.

"Are you eating properly? Are you looking for a job?" I ask.

Brian tells me that Troy is doing various drugs, that the
girl he is with is young and stupid but hopelessly in love with
him. I try to believe that he wants more than this from his

life. I believe that if I love him enough and in just the right
way, he will come back to me and we will be happy again, together. But he doesn't come back, despite my best efforts to
convince him.

With the help of a real estate agent who makes house
calls, I buy a house and get ready to move soon. I am excited
about this fresh start. The house will be a new beginning for
me. All day I imagine the view of the ocean, the garden I will
cultivate. I love it, though it will be just me, alone to grieve
the past two years of my life. From the house I can walk to the
ocean to go swimming. Some things are coming together.

I pray a lot now. I need God's guidance, and I count my
blessings for the people—Juli, my mom, Paul, my dad, my
sister, my employers, Donna, and even Troy—who have seen
me through the worst time in my life.

I have two more months of house arrest. Now that I am
truly alone, I find a measure of resolve, a core of steel. With
two months left, I apply through the court for a change in my
conditional sentence. "I'll support you in making the change,"
my supervisor says.

I fill out the forms with ease, noting that I now live by
myself with a dog to care for, that I have exceeded my community volunteer hours at the SPCA, and that I am requesting
a change from complete house arrest to a curfew, which would
allow me to go to the bank and take Seymour for walks after
work. The court administrator has never seen an offender-
generated request before and has to look up the procedure in a
four-inch-thick manual. She looks at me strangely. It is more
common for a probation officer to file these papers, trying to
get an offender's conditions made more restrictive. A hearing
date is set for January 29, 2001.

Entering the court, I feel a now-familiar anxiety. In the waiting room, Sue, my supervisor, says, "I just found out that the Crown is going to oppose your request." My heart sinks. How can I argue against a lawyer with years of legal training? Perhaps I should just give up, turn around, get back in my car, and drive home. But I am here, and this is the only chance I have, however small, to improve my life. I am still debating whether to run out of there when the large swinging doors to the court open and my name is called.

Repeating to myself that I am initiating this action, and that if I don't remain strong I may end up hanging from the rafters of my house, I stand before the judge. I speak first, presenting my case for the change in sentence to the judge, my voice wavering and my hands shaking in the most unlitigious manner.

When I finish, Crown counsel rises and says, "Your Honor, the Crown opposes this change." She goes on to explain that there is no substantial reason to reduce my sentence, that it should be served in its entirety.

"Hmmm," Judge Giroday begins. "Well, I see that Ms. Ingram is not requesting an early release from her sentence, only a change to an 8:00 P.M. curfew." The judge asks me a few questions about the size of my yard and then asks whether I have any family in Gibsons.

"No," I say.

"The court grants Ms. Ingram this change," she proclaims. With a smack of her gavel, she leaves the room, and I sit stunned. I won. Behind me, Juli is already crying, and soon we are hugging each other and crying together. I can walk out of the building and go get a cup of coffee legally. Oh my God. I can buy groceries tonight!

"I'm so proud of you," Juli says. We relive each moment of the morning aloud, laughing and crying the whole ride home.

When I leave work the next day, I force my feet from their usual path home and head down to the beach. The late-afternoon sun is low above the smooth gray ocean. Finding a log, I sit and look and breathe—alone, but free. Everything around me looks beautiful, seems poignant, as if I am seeing it for the first time. There are new shades of gray in the sand, the sky. I feel a small puddle of joy in my stomach. Is this what freedom feels like? But I am only partly free.

And then it hits me with full force. I am out, but my life from before is gone, as are most of my friends, my career, my place in the community. It is simply not there to be picked up again. I think about my former students and feel an enormous sense of loss, a loss of my privilege of involvement in their futures. I think about teaching, and how every day I miss it with all my heart. I think about the friends who no longer speak to me—about Mark, about Joanne, about Vivian—and about the other teachers at Chatelech. I think about Troy and wish he were here to share this moment with me. I had been sure that being outside on the beach would feel good, but right now I feel overwhelmed by sadness. What I have done is big and irreversible.

Reading about issues and observing others has always been enough to teach me that I didn't want to smoke, that I wanted to do well in school, that my sense of self did not depend on my dress size or the color of my hair. But I have had to learn some things the hard way. That loving people, for example, is a responsibility, and that accepting yourself and others is the foundation of that responsibility. Troy tried to teach me, but I couldn't learn fast enough to save us. I am alone on this beach today because of my own actions. The ache in my heart is my teacher.

Knowing that I was in court this morning, Troy calls after work. "How did it go?"

"Great! I got it!"

"Congratulations," he says. It feels good to talk to him with happiness in my voice. It feels so good to be a little bit free, and I wonder in the back of my mind if this will give us an opportunity to be together again on more equal footing.

"Let's go have dinner and celebrate," I suggest.

"Sounds good."

As the weeks go by, he is around me more and more. I naïvely believe that we can go back to the way we were, that if we have enough fun together he will forget about his young girlfriend and be with me instead. Sunday afternoons we go ice skating or off-roading with friends. We sit side by side in the backseat, Troy's arm curled tentatively around my shoulder. The motion of the truck pushes us closer together. Laughter, shrieks. We are having fun.

As darkness settles low across the black trees one evening, I get nervous about the time. "I've got to be home before eight," I remind everyone. Troy sighs. I read a world in that sigh, a world of late nights, drugs, and young girls, the days distinguished only by which video is playing on the VCR.

Purposefully light, I say, "I saw a roofing job in the paper today. Interested?"

He looks at me as if he would like to unload the weight of the past month. "Yeah."

"I wish that you loved me," I say suddenly.

He looks surprised, and with rare force says, "Heather, I love you so much it scares me."

I have to ask the next question. *"Why* does it scare you?"

He is quiet for a long time, and the music from the front seat suddenly becomes louder. "Because I can give myself up for you."

The similarities to my past thoughts about Mark are eerie. I don't know what to say. I am struck by his self-awareness and by his unwillingness to give himself up for anyone. I feel humbled, put in my place. With new respect, I squeeze his hand.

A FEW WEEKS LATER, I take Seymour out to Smuggler's Cove for a long oceanside walk. On the way back through Sechelt, I notice a police car behind me. Suddenly its lights start flashing. I pull over, scared, but also indignant. I wasn't speeding. I recognize this officer; it's Constable Rosenberg again, and immediately I feel sick to my stomach, remembering his treatment of Troy.

In the parking lot next to my car a small crowd of people is gathering. Brian is there, and Andrew, and even Daniel, whom I haven't seen in over a year. Rosenberg asks to see my driver's licence and a copy of my conditional sentence order, which I must carry with me at all times. I hand the paperwork to him, saying, "You know that I received a change in my sentence, to a curfew. My supervisor said that she notified the RCMP in Gibsons."

"Well, you're in Sechelt now," he says, and I feel a wave of dislike for this man. But he is just doing his job, I remind myself, no matter how humiliating this is. He makes me wait by my car for about five minutes. When he finally hands back my paperwork with a curt, "Good enough for me," I feel debased. My day is ruined; I feel subhuman again. The crowd in the parking lot is joking and laughing.

Everywhere I go in this town, people know me and recognize my face. This embarrassing spectacle has been a brutal reminder of my status as "other."

Just when I gain a bit of self-respect, it is always taken from me. I know that I can brush this situation off if I choose, but the indignity of the system infuriates me. Yes, I committed a crime, but to actively reinforce the low self-esteem that made that crime possible seems ludicrous. It is happening to me, where I live, in front of people I know. I am trying hard to rebuild my life, but every board I nail down can be ripped apart by an arbitrary building inspector. It all seems so futile. I sink down in my seat as I drive the rest of the way home.

# 19

# Rehabilitation

*M*ARCH 29, 2001. Freedom day, I have been calling it, as I cross each day off on my calendar. Ten months of Xs.

It is a day like any other. I go to work, and after work I walk home, drop my bag in the hallway, and turn on the hot water in the bathtub.

Tonight Troy and I are planning to go out for a drink to celebrate. Since he got the roofing job last month he has been with me almost every night, telling me he loves me, gradually moving his stuff into my house again. In the morning I make his lunch and send him to work. I assume he has broken up with his girlfriend; we are together most of the time, and when I ask he tells me that he does not see her at all, something I will find out later is a lie. I am happy, glad to have him back, but also busy growing into myself and remembering how to be out in public again, shopping and going to

movies. If becoming an adult is truly understanding the consequences of your actions, then for the first time, at thirty-
one, I am an adult.

ONE FRIDAY NIGHT in late April I suddenly wake up. It's
about 1:30 A.M. Why am I awake? I just have time to look
on the other side of the bed and realize that Troy is not
here, as he said he would be, before the phone rings. His
voice is in my ear, shaky and frightened, incoherent. "Oh
my God, oh my God."

"Troy, what's happened?"

"I had an accident. Can you come get me?"

"Where are you?" I think about that night almost two
years ago when he phoned and asked me to do the same thing.

"I don't know—the Shores—I don't know. Oh my God . . ."

"OK, I'll be right there."

The Shores is a wealthy housing development out in
Sechelt. I'm not sure how I'll find him, but I get in my car
and drive towards it, peering through the dark for indications
of an accident. My heart is pounding, my senses alert.

Within half an hour I see an ambulance turning the corner
towards the hospital. Its lights aren't flashing—is that a good
sign or . . . ? I can't think of it. Continuing in the direction
the ambulance came from, I soon see four police cars and
about fifteen people standing around. I pull over well before
the scene and start walking towards it.

When Troy sees me, he reaches forward and embraces me,
leaning down on my shoulders with all his weight. My arms
hang down; I don't hug him back. I can smell the pot smoke
on him; I can imagine the reckless speed with which he has

been driving. Are you having fun yet, Troy? He reads the judgment in my face, his cheeks still tear-stained, and I can tell that
he feels rebuked, unacceptable to me once again.

He says, "Do you at least want to see the car?" He takes me
to a steep driveway overlooking a spectacular ocean view. In
the driveway his recently purchased black Camaro is upside
down, having flipped off the road. Concrete blocks from the
retaining wall have smashed down with the car. He would have
come around the corner of this quiet residential neighborhood
and lost it over the edge of the wall. His shoulder, shredded,
black and red, peers through the torn fabric of his shirt.

Now a police officer is walking over to talk to Troy. Without a word, I go back to my car and sit behind the wheel,
watching them talk. The night is cool and I am shaking.
Troy's driving companions come and sit with me in the car.
Scott, a former student, tells me, "They took Brian to the hospital. They think he has a concussion." The boys are reliving
the accident, describing coming around the corner, the lift,
the descent, the slide, getting out of the vehicle through the
broken back window, their conversation with a neighbor who
told them that he had already called the police.

When Troy finally finishes his conversation with the police, he is issued a narrow slip of yellow paper with a reckless
driving charge on it and a twenty-four-hour licence suspension. I take him directly to the hospital. Brian, still drunk,
has been released, and Troy is lying on a metal bed while a
bearded, jovial doctor picks rocks out of his shoulder with a
set of tweezers.

"Are you mad at me?" he asks, wincing and gritting his
teeth whenever the tweezers probe his bleeding flesh.

"I'm not mad, just disappointed in you," I say quietly. "You could have killed yourself, or one of your friends." He looks away. "Here, squeeze my hand, Troy." He takes my hand. When the doctor tells him "Hold on tight," and begins to swab the wound with an antiseptic, he braces his body, clenches his teeth, but his hand will not squeeze mine tight. His breathing is shallow and hoarse. Tears leak from his eyes—tears that have been months in coming. His aquamarine eyes are rimmed with red. The doctor gives him some Tylenol 3s and sends him home with me.

By the time we get back to my house, it is almost 4:00 A.M. I feel like a mother, the mother I never had and never have been; I'm needed and happy to be needed. I lay him into the clean sheets of my bed. He curls around me, almost fetal, and hangs on, sobbing. "I fucked up," he whispers. "I fucked up so badly."

I pull him tighter against me. "Yes," I whisper back. "Be grateful you lived to learn the lesson."

My heart is twisted up with his. We pull ourselves closer to each other, wounds raw, trying to touch our insides together. I know that tomorrow he will be fine, excitedly describing the accident over and over to his friends, enjoying the attention, showing them his wounds—they're already knitting themselves into a great story. Tonight, though, he is with me, his vulnerability large and beautiful, his tough exterior dissolved. Love, need, it's all the same to us. Our bodies do not relax until sleep comes.

WHEN SUMMER LIFTS THE SUN HIGHER, Troy is still working for the roofing company, although the work is not steady and he is constantly strapped for money. I give him forty dollars here and there as I can squeeze it out. He seems grateful for the donations, and always hugs me tight, but there is a wounded pride in his eyes.

Most days he goes off to Sechelt while I go to work. When I ask him what he has done during the day I get either "worked" or "nothing," depending on whether his boss has called or not. Mornings are stressful, as we lie in bed and wait for the eight o'clock phone call. Business is slow. More often than not, there is no work, and on my lunch breaks I comb the meager want ads in the local paper for him. Even the highly paid mill workers are losing their jobs. For someone like me, with years of education and lots of computer skills, it is tough. For someone like Troy, who hasn't even finished high school, the situation is grave.

I need a break. I arrange for a few days off work so that Juli and I can drive to the Merritt Mountain Music Festival, a four-day country music/camping/drinking gathering of thousands in the interior of B.C. Campers and RVs are packed in endless rows. The grass is gray, dry and dusty. The guy in the RV next to us dumps generous portions of Baileys Irish Cream into our morning coffees. Grasshoppers jump as I step from Juli's Jeep into the main field.

I can't remember seeing this many young people in one place before. Everyone looks under thirty, drunk, happy, and ready to party, and almost everyone is good looking. "Yup," Lisa says when Juli and I meet up with her. "If you want to get laid this weekend, this is the place." She weaves her way through the throngs of people towards the beer garden bar. Before she even makes it, a man with no shirt and rubber boots is hitting on her.

In the river there are lawn chairs stacked six deep. A man floats by with a plastic cup holder duct-taped to his inner tube. Girls lie face down on air mattresses, laughing, arching their backs so that their wet bikini bottoms reveal their firm round buttocks. I don't know what to do or how to be in this environment.

Juli and I sit on the bank of the river watching the scene around us, people our age, presumably most without criminal records, shrieking and splashing and laughing. A guy with a megaphone in one hand and a Kokanee in the other provides a running commentary on each person who tries to cross the thigh-deep river. A girl on the bank rips her shirt off to thunderous applause and cheers. I sit with my book, reading the same paragraph over and over, watching the scene around me, feeling removed from these people. Is this what normal looks like? Although I don't fit in with Troy's social circle, I am no closer to fitting in here, with people my own age. A Frisbee flies by in front of me, and two girls tackle a guy wearing bright yellow flowered shorts. They laugh loudly as they roll on the grassy riverbank.

I don't feel normal. I can't scream and play and splash water around. The damage is done and done deep. Don't these people know that this world can all be taken away? Don't they know how fragile the illusion is, that the road check when they drive home tonight could land them in jail, that their drunken trip to the river at midnight could end in a stumble, a fall, a drowning, or that the sex they have tonight could land them in the hospital or worse? Danger is every-where—in this field, on the highway driving home. As Troy said after he saw the burned man last summer, life is precious, and I will never be able to un-know it. I almost wish that I could forget for a weekend how tenuous life is, because then maybe I could enjoy it.

JULI IS STILL TRYING to find me a social life. She points out that my shoulders are rounded. I also look at the ground when I walk, my eyes darting to the side to check for people who might know me. Even my clothes are darker, less adventurous. Has it really been two years since that night with Daniel when I felt like a goddess, like my own person, as if my life was finally beginning? It is hard to remember that feeling. When she sees me, Juli's eyes cloud over.

On a rare night out at the bar, I find myself next to a twenty-two-year-old young man named Dave, whose girlfriend is flirting with another guy. He looks miserable. He makes a gallant attempt to be polite, asking dispiritedly, "So . . . what's new?"

Why do we deny that we are in pain? I have lost the ability to make small talk, which is a liability in most situations. People either like it or hate it when you tell them the truth. "I'm sorry. I don't do small talk," I say, not rudely, but firmly.

"All right," he says bravely, as if he is stepping off a curb into traffic. "What do you want to talk about?"

I pause a moment, not expecting him to play the ball back to me, wondering what I *do* want to talk about. "OK," I say, "what's important to you? Top three. Don't think about it, just speak."

After a short breath out, Dave says, "Family. Fidelity. Money." I smile. He looks relieved, and his shoulders drop half an inch. "What's important to you?" he asks.

I have no idea what will come out of my mouth in the next few seconds. "Love. Acceptance. Fulfillment."

"Those are good choices," he says.

On a cool Saturday morning in July, I board the forty-minute ferry to Vancouver. I am starting to get over my terror at being recognized, but my eyes automatically scan the seats of people to determine who I know, who I should avoid. I pick an inconspicuous spot near the front and lean my head back against the cool vinyl headrest. With my iBook open in front of me, I can ignore the people walking by, ignore the high-pitched social chatter of the elderly women sitting behind me. In my peripheral vision suddenly there is someone familiar; he plops his body down in the seat opposite me and extends his legs across the space between us, crossing his feet on the seat beside me. "Hi," he says.

"Josh," I reply, "Wow, I haven't seen you in a while. How are you?" Josh graduated from Chatelech the year before I left. We spent some time back then talking about his mom's RRSPs, and I remember him telling me that she had cancer.

He looks at me quizzically. "Do you really want to know?"

"Of course," I say.

"My mom died last month. It's been tough." His voice is matter of fact, but there is pain in his eyes. He is only twenty-one. What must the last month have been like for him?

"Tell me about it."

"Honestly?" Josh asks earnestly. "There aren't many people who want to hear this shit. It's pretty ugly."

I nod, feeling a part of myself open across the green patterned carpet between us. "You know, people who have been through pain recognize it immediately in other people," I tell him. "That means that I only care about stuff that's real."

Josh relaxes, and begins to open up to me about his mother's death, her funeral, the upheaval in his life. Listening to him, I am struck by the difference between the student I knew in class and the mature young man before me who is weathering a serious storm. He is right; the picture is brutal. I am grateful to be sitting here, one person with another, murmuring my compassion, trying to convey my empathy. The definition of student that has been so critical to my court case evaporates in the face of the human response we give each other during this brief ferry ride to Vancouver. We exchange phone numbers, and hug as the ferry docks. "It's been really good to see you," he whispers in my ear.

"You too," I say.

EACH DAY I CAN FEEL Troy growing more distant from me. It has been three years since our relationship began. His voice is deeper and his neck is thicker; more hairs have sprouted on his chest. His emotions are evolving too, and I feel out of my league, inadequate to guide him in this process. And he seems to want my guidance less and less. He complains to me, as he used to complain to his mom, "You're always telling me what to do." Just as he did this time last year, he is going out more, although he calls and leaves me loving messages on my answering machine. "I'll be home tonight. I love you. Please don't be mad." He is quicker than ever before in his anger when I question him as to his whereabouts. He seems on edge. I read books about boys' maturation process, trying to find ways to talk to him about his life. I read that eighty percent of the males in jail are the children of single mothers, that the boys who join gangs are those who have no positive male role models. Some of this learning I share with Troy. I say, "I just read that boys need a tribe."

"Yeah," he says, hoping that I can begin to understand him. "Yeah, you need to read more stuff like that."

In the meantime, my suspicions are running wild. I begin to run my hands through his jacket pockets and sneak out to check the glove compartment of his car. One morning while he is asleep upstairs, I search through his wallet, feeling sharp pangs of guilt mixed with desperation. I am searching for something that will tell me what is really going on, but of course I do not want to find anything.

Really, I am searching for answers. Why do I feel so alone, even though you're right here? Why don't we talk anymore? Where do you go during your day? Why am I so scared? Inside his wallet I find many small scraps of paper: "Mitch 752-8923" or "Buddy 868-2359." No girls' names appear, but I do not know who these men are. If they are his friends, I've never met them. Also folded into separate compartments of his wallet are bills, a few fifties, more twenties—not a lot, but enough. I calculate how much firewood he has been cutting lately and whether this could account for the money. Dimly, I am aware that this is not the way a relationship should be or how I want ours to be.

Inside both of us there is something that made us able to cross the line from teacher and student to lovers. Now, that same thing, the need to feel loved, the belief that love can surmount all obstacles, is keeping us together but burying us. I do the only thing I know how to do—pull harder, question him fiercely. Something is desperately wrong, but I don't know what it is. At bottom is the suspicion that he is lying, he is living a life that he is concealing from me. He tells me just enough truth to keep me from pushing for more.

My bosses give me relationship advice, about setting boundaries and what a healthy relationship looks like. I can understand this concept, but it is like looking through Plexiglas at a dance performance. There are colors, and people moving around, but they are removed. From Mark to Troy, it's a span of almost fifteen years, and I have not learned how to be happy in a relationship.

I remember my friend Joanne telling me, "People will deny something for as long as they can." As we hang lights and pick out a Christmas tree, our rituals feel hollow, surface. "Are you still seeing her?" I ask, hazarding a guess that the girl he was with at the beginning of the year is still around.

"Sometimes I see her walking down the street," he says. "But that's all."

Out at the bar late one Saturday night, Christine pulls me aside. "You need to hear this," she says, and suddenly I know what she is going to say. "He's still sleeping with Steph. I'm so sorry, Heather."

Knowing that there is no way he will tell me the truth, I pick a night when he is not home and sit in the elementary school parking lot across from her house. Within half an hour, I see his car pull up and he drops her off. I feel stricken, and yet a part of me welcomes the familiar feeling of doom. This too can fall away, along with all my other illusions. Yes, it is good. I am stripping furniture, the heavy shards of paint curling and floating towards the floor, the tart smell of turpentine rising around me.

With a heavy mass in my stomach, my chest constricted, I follow him into a gas station and confront him with what I have just seen. I put my hand sideways on his chest, covering his heart, willing him to feel the connection that has sustained us for almost three years.

"What? Who's feeding you this bullshit?" he says angrily, looking around to see who is watching, avoiding my eyes.

My heart is beating at twice its normal rate. His eyes look scared, but his face is still cloaked in denial. "I saw you," I breathe to him, lifting my palm so that my fingertips are resting lightly on his chest. And I see now that it is true.

"You've been sleeping with her?" I ask.

"Yes," he whispers painfully, and looks toward the sky. There is a silence that seems to take forever. "She's easy to be with," he breathes, as if this explanation can be enough. Yet I know that this statement encompasses everything for him. I am not easy to be with. I criticize him, his friends, his pot smoking, his lifestyle. I am afraid of being pulled over by the police; I do not want to go to raucous, drug-filled parties. We are so different; I knew this from the beginning. How naïve to think that love could overcome not only all that we have been through but our differences too. A whole year of lies confronts me. I remember our evening standing on Les's boat and watching the fish jump. I would give anything, would go through everything I've been through again, for us to feel that way once more.

It takes all my strength to give him back the ring I have worn for over a year and without a word leave him standing at the gas station. The next day when I return from work his things are gone from my house. The crystal heart he gave me for Christmas is smashed on my tiled entrance—there are no sweet crystal possibilities left. Everything that is unsaid between us haunts me. I lie on the couch, too wretched to cry. I don't even know this person. Maybe he doesn't even know himself. I clutch my sides and try to squeeze the pain out of me. Almost three years to the day, and it is finally over. The ending, the beginning, who knows. I have learned so much and have so much more to learn. I am more lonely than I have ever been and yet so much more myself.

I recall every sensation: kissing the tears from his eyelashes the night he rolled his car; his body curling around me while I lay in bed sobbing the night I confessed our relationship to my principal; walking down the steps from the courtroom with his arm bracing me from falling; his strong arms play-wrestling with me in the living room while I was under house arrest. I press my face into Seymour's warm head and close my eyes, wishing to undo, wishing to be undone.

# 20

# 49/51

BY ALL APPEARANCES I am back in society. I have a respectable full-time job, I have friends, and my little house is gradually sprouting a garden. People I don't know ask me who designed my house, which feels so much like me that I couldn't have asked for anything better. I am friendly with them, and they are friendly back, although I am told that everyone in this neighborhood knows who I am. It is left unspoken between us, this knowledge.

The people in my life who like me but don't know me well—the gas station attendant, the post office clerks, the couple who lives down the street—consider my relationship with Troy an error in judgment, as if I had driven home from a party one night after three glasses of wine. "You just made a mistake," they say, nodding with compassion and embracing me back into society as if the consequences I have faced were merely a bad hangover.

But it is not that simple. They do not see the difference between us, which perhaps has always been there, or might be the difference between reading the newspaper and being the news itself. I still don't look like a criminal, not even to myself. Sometimes when I am out for lunch with girlfriends and the topic of my experience comes up, I say the words "convicted sex offender" and watch the shock and then the recognition on their faces as they realize that these words apply to me, somebody they call a friend.

I feel different too, and I wonder if this difference will grow or disappear as the time since Troy left for good increases. I am marked as different not only by my mistake but by my mistrust of people who buy fully into society's conventions. People who ignore the underside of life, who withhold compassion and offer judgment instead, are not my friends—though I will be friendly to them on the street. Those who have not been through something publicly traumatic do not understand why I cannot be detached about the news. The two men at the restaurant who argued about my case while I sat a few tables away are firmly implanted in my memory: "He knew what he was doing. She succumbed to him. What seventeen-year-old guy wouldn't sleep with his teacher if given half a chance?" "No, no way. She had a responsibility to resist. I say put her away."

I remember the psychologist who evaluated me as part of my sentence, asking me, really, didn't I enjoy all the media attention? I looked at him as if he were the crazy one and asked if he would like to be trapped in his house, unable by court order to leave, with reporters knocking at his door, creeping around the back of the house, and peering in the windows. These experiences mark me as different forever.

An acquaintance does not understand why I don't want her to find me a nice, "appropriate" thirty-something career man. Why would I not want someone to mark me as fully reinstated, fully rehabilitated? But I am afraid of that smothered feeling I had with Mark, of losing myself again in a relationship, of relying too much on rules and structures, of feeling like I can never live up to someone's standards. I don't want to apologize anymore for who I am.

But there is more than that. Part of me is angry. Why would I would want to go back into society—a society I now see as created and perpetuated by people who are predominantly unhappy but who have invested so much time, energy, and money in creating the illusion of the ideal way of living that they must keep up that illusion? A girlfriend describes how she kept her impending divorce a secret from her best friend for months, how she kept her pain and sorrow and fear closed up securely inside her, mainly because she felt ashamed. She had failed to live up to an institutional ideal and felt that she would be judged harshly for it, by her friend and maybe by herself.

Some of the trappings of society are good—my home, for example. Knocked down, I have a deeply seated instinct to rebuild. I feel proud of myself for having the strength to put things back together after I lost my home, my partner, my career, my reputation, my clean record, my privacy. I still live in the same small town, and the reminders of the past three years are constant, and sometimes hilarious. One day the softball team I play for competes against the RCMP team, and Constable Rosenberg, instead of pulling me over, is pitching to me. But it is easy to be here: I stay because I can own a house, have a large dog, and enjoy the beaches all summer. It is also strangely safe, because I don't have to explain my situation; most people already know the story.

My middle-class veneer has been stripped off. As Troy's friend Andrew (now my friend too) says to me ominously, "You're one of us now." He means that I am no longer a teacher, but he also means that I am no longer one of "them"—those who live in well-to-do houses (not trailers) and have professional jobs and formal education and families who cook ten side dishes with their turkey for Thanksgiving dinner each year. When I explain that my chances of going back to my old world are small, he just shrugs, and says, "Everybody has a criminal record." And here on the Sunshine Coast, among people he knows, most do. I want to tell him that no, that's not true, that most people go through their entire lives thinking of "that" type of people, which now includes me, as opposed to "their" type of people. I am finally getting the education I needed.

Another one of Troy's friends says, "I don't really understand your motivation." We are sitting around my oak dining room table; I feel lucky that many of Troy's friends still come to see me and are my friends now too. He is drinking beer from a can; I have a bottle of Mike's Hard Lemonade. "You have a *legitimate* life," he says, frowning. "Why are you hanging out with us?"

I want to tell him that I am motivated by the complexity of life's choices, by honesty, pain, and love. But I know that this won't make any sense to him. I want to describe how I found some of these things in moments with Troy. An overcast afternoon spent collecting shells together at low tide, discovering new salty life forms, is precious. So is sitting in my backyard at 2:00 A.M., sleepy and cold, holding hands with Troy and watching a meteor shower, feeling sheer wonder. I am caught in between the appearance of a smooth, calm surface and the cauldron of feelings that lies beneath it.

Many of Troy's friends don't even believe that a legitimate life is possible for them, that they deserve it or could ever achieve it. And yet here I am, having built such a life, not only once but twice, and still choosing to spend time with them. By accepting the complexity of their lives, giving them a place to be honest, listening to the pain, and trying to give love, I feel good about myself. I still have something to give. I am still "teaching," my students older but still alternate; they have no insulation from the world, no padding of wealth or social standing. They are raw, unfinished, open. Through each one of them I am reminded of what's important in life.

My teacher identity lives on in these twenty-something young adults. My influence is there, minor, but still alive. "Ms. Ingram . . . I mean, *Heather,*" Charlotte giggles when she greets me in a store. Most of them are used to calling me that now. I have a weakness for people who confess, as one of my alternate students did late one night at a back table of the local bar, "I love learning." This statement comes with a mild look of shock, as if he can't quite believe it himself. I remember briefly that this is the same young man who arrived silent and angry one day in my Accounting 11 class, flashing a straight razor blade around to his friends.

Strangely, people from my old life are calling me again. I feel as if I have a sign on my forehead that says, "Confess your darkest secrets here." Friends I haven't heard from in years suddenly want to know how I am, want to get together for coffee. What do I have to offer them? They come with compassion and with questions. Katherine, her voice from two years ago still ringing in my head—"Happy? Who's happy?"— tells me about the last six months of her life. "One day I woke up in my beautiful three-thousand-square-foot house with its high ceilings and designer kitchen and thought, I'm not having any fun. I'm working sixty hours a week. All my relationships are superficial. It's like we're keeping up some pretense so that everybody can feel good about the hell they're in." She sighs heavily.

I don't feel like some guru with answers to give them. Most days I can only see as far as sundown. Yet I feel blessed to be able to help people in minor but critical ways. All around me people are in pain. My compassion feels endless and deep. I listen and provide encouragement. I am still a teacher after all.

I can't remember the exact day in the past six months that I stopped being afraid to go to the mall or to walk down the main street of Sechelt and walk into a store. This time a year ago, I can remember my heart pounding, my fingers twitching, my stomach twisted in panic, my shoulders stooped in shame. Yet today a trim man close to fifty is making his way to my table one night at a restaurant, and introducing himself as Becky's dad. I remember that he is the owner of this establishment and that we played mixed doubles tennis in my former life. He is exactly the type of person I would expect not to talk to me anymore. He crouches down and leans in so that I can hear him above the noise around us. "I wanted to thank you for teaching Becky," he says. We talk about how she is doing, and I remember him and his wife about four years ago sitting in

the gym for parent-teacher interviews, despairing, not knowing what to do, looking to me for advice. Now Becky is
doing great.

"She's a smart girl," I tell him, and he looks pleased. "You're
home free." He smiles, nodding; the struggle is worth it.

Now, as I move into the next phase of my life, I want to
use what I've learned from Troy. Through him I learned that
your self is all you have, that nobody can take that from you,
that relationships can feel good, that it's not OK to take out
your frustration with life on your partner, and that being
judgmental about people closes you off from new experiences.
Mostly he stretched me in ways that I didn't even know it was
possible to grow. Thanks to him, almost nothing shocks me
anymore. Three years ago, I could form opinions on things,
identify right and wrong, assign blame with ease. Now the
shades of gray are infinite. I get lost in the complexity.

I feel Troy's absence every minute. It hurts to hear that he
is renting a place of his own, that he is cooking and washing
his own clothes, that he doesn't need me anymore, that he
has moved on. It would hurt more, I remind myself, to hear
that he was not able to do these things, and I remember to
celebrate his growth, even if it is without me. Growth is bio-
logical, irrefutable, and nobody can be saved from it. Those
books about goals and plans that I was so fond of under house
arrest make me laugh now. I no longer want to map out a five-
year plan and then achieve it, or live for the future. My life, as
different as it is from what I anticipated, is now, and I want to
make it the best it can be.

For a few months after our breakup, Troy would come to see
me, usually on Sunday afternoons. He would knock awkwardly

on the same door he used to breeze through, and he would fish around for the ashtray lying unused at the back of my kitchen shelf. I would offer food, which he ate with enthusiasm, and then we would sit on the couch, his head on my lap, one arm curled around my waist. Sometimes he would talk about his life; more often he would simply fall into a sleep that felt deep and necessary. A few hours later, fortified, he would leave, as if he were a soldier going back to the front, the front line of growth, independence, change. He does not come by much anymore; he doesn't need me in this way. Yet I want to save him still. I want to grab his shoulders and say, "I love you. Please take care of yourself." But I will try to accept him no matter what. It is what we all want from each other, and what we can rarely give.

What was it all for? My picture is sometimes in the paper still, whenever another teacher is dismissed for misconduct, with the single-word caption "Disgraced," media shorthand for all that I have gone through. Am I merely a pathetic loss, my life and career a write-off? I don't believe that. The losses aren't as important to me as they once were. I still miss teaching, but a surprising number of local parents pay me to tutor math to their teenagers, which has rewards of its own. People's opinions don't matter as much. Change is painful, but the compassion I've gained as a result is good. When I look out my window now, even if I am alone, I am OK.

On a night out for a drive with Brian, we bounce down a gravel road, the headlights spotlighting the potholes to avoid. Brian is getting ready to move to Calgary to go to school. The move scares him and makes every moment before it poignant. "You taught me something," he says above the music, as our bodies jostle with the motion of the truck. "You taught me that you can lose everything, but as long as you still believe in yourself, you're OK."

I know that the line between lying to yourself and believing in something is thin, but I don't say that to Brian. Instead, I hug him around his shoulders, while tears form behind my smile. The real reward of teaching is being a part of somebody's learning. I still have that.

I was charged and pleaded guilty to one count of Canadian Criminal Code Section 153, Sexual Exploitation of a Minor, the mildest of the sexual offences. I abused my privilege as a teacher, and for that I have lost my teaching license and will never again be allowed to teach in a public school or work with anyone under the age of eighteen. My criminal record will prevent me from getting many other jobs and from traveling to the United States. I spent ten months under house arrest and completed 120 hours of community service and another twelve months of probation.

A man I know told me that I might have been able to avoid a criminal record if I had pleaded not guilty and proceeded with a trial, as other female teachers have done since my case. But I do not regret my decision. After much soul searching, I have concluded that I did not exploit Troy, that I did not in any way coerce him into our relationship. I believe that he knew what he was doing when he pursued me, that he did love me, and that for a short while we had a relationship that was sweet and wonderful.

Did I damage Troy? Absolutely. I expected far too much adult decision-making from someone who had not yet turned eighteen. I neglected to realize how much he idealized me and how much my infidelity with Daniel damaged him. I also deprived him of a part of his youth. Did I abuse my power as a teacher? In the strictest sense, yes. I ignored that power and chose to believe that I could simply be a person in love with someone eleven years my junior, that somehow things would work out. Although I didn't know that I could face a criminal charge for our relationship, I did understand that the consequences of my actions would be bad. Yet I did everything in my power to show him alternatives too, to encourage him to work hard and continue his education. Sometimes I feel hurt that he still does not value these things as much as I do.

I believe it was low self-esteem that enabled me to cross the teacher-student line and betray my professional responsibility as I did. I took on too much responsibility too young and missed most of the social learning that teenagers gain. As a kid I felt good but not good enough and pretended that appearances didn't matter because I felt ugly. The truth is that I wanted to be pretty and popular as well as smart, like other girls. I tried to compensate for my family's deficiencies by proving that I could be successful and in control, by achieving high marks in school, by trying to meet all of Mark's expectations. By the time I realized that I couldn't, it was too late and I was with someone who, like me, didn't know how to get himself unstuck from his childhood patterns. We tried to use our house and careers to achieve happiness, but they were only surrogates. I began to hate feeling chronically unworthy in my relationship with Mark, to the point that I was ready to do almost anything to get rid of the feeling.

With Troy I felt sexual and desirable. I got to experience freedom to try things I'd never tried before, and permission to

explore being a teenager, which I found irresistible. I deeply regret that we began our relationship when Troy was my student.
If I had waited until he left school, much of the damage I
caused to myself and the school would not have happened. I do
not regret loving Troy; for me that part was real and important. I would *like* to say that I would not do it all again if I
could relive the past, but given my emotional state at the
time I can't be sure. What I do know is that I would not
make the same mistake now. Most of the time I don't feel
like a bad person; but I still beat myself up on occasion for
my short-sightedness and naïveté.

I regret the damage I did to Mark too, but ultimately the
experience has been beneficial for him. We connect by e-mail
and the occasional phone call; he tells me that he wasn't happy
either back then, and though loneliness still winds through
him, he is happier now. He has carried on with the renovations
in what used to be our house, and e-mails me about the new
dishwasher or the hardwood floors finally installed three years
after I left. I rejoice in knowing that our dream is living on
through his efforts. I recall our past together in a faint, neutral
way, without much emotion. The times we went camping, our
struggles and arguments, the months he spent in Hudson's
Hope, my tears over rewiring the baseboard heater, sitting beside him on the flowered bedspread that ski weekend I told
him about Troy—these moments are faded for me. They are
veiled behind the past three years of experiences we have not
shared, ones that have made me into an adult. If only I could
have said, "Mark, something needs to change; I'm not happy,"
we might have avoided causing each other so much pain. But
some learnings come too late.

I feel good knowing that I was honest about my relationship with Troy after the pressure of carrying on the deception for ten months became too great; I tried as much as possible to behave honorably after the fact and to take my punishment, one that turned out to be far greater and more far-reaching than I could have imagined. Do I regret telling Vivian? Not really, in the end. I learned that fear is a powerful motivator, that you should never assume someone will be loyal to you, that you cannot predict what another person will do, especially when they have something to lose.

I am grateful for the people who are still with me, the ones who have the courage to acknowledge me in the mall, the ones who have the guts to admit that they didn't know how to handle it when I showed up on the front page and wish they could have been there for me, the ones who come up to me these days and wish me well.

When Vivian and I met for coffee that Sunday back in October 1999, I still had a CD she had lent me at home. Jewel. I still cannot listen to Jewel on the radio without thinking of Vivian and of that intense time in my life. There is a line from that album that seems more beautiful and more true as I get older. "In the end, only kindness matters . . ." I remember the people in my life who are no longer in my life—Joanne, Daniel, my teaching colleagues. It seems, finally, that I have only kindness to give and to receive. It is my role in life not to be great or famous or rich but to find kindness, to listen, to love in my own inadequate way, to be hurt when that love is not reciprocated, and to keep loving anyway.

I wish I could be sure that I will be loved again as I was loved once by Troy. I wish I could feel good about myself no matter what anybody thinks, but this will always be a struggle for me. I walk through the woods behind my house and smell the sun baking the cedar chips, pick my way over the fallen logs, feel the mud drying hard beneath my feet, notice the sharp difference in temperature between the light and dark spaces in this small piece of second-growth forest. I think about Troy, and I bless him on his path of growth. I try each moment to force out the loneliness that whips under the space between my shirt and my jacket and around the bare skin at my ankles.

I hope that one day when many years have passed we will have a cup of coffee and catch up on each other's life. I try to imagine him at thirty, at forty, with two kids in school. I hope we are able to hug and to laugh. I wonder who he will become, and if I will still know him. One thing is for sure, I am not interested in illusions anymore. Reality is interesting, sustaining, and more rewarding than any happily-ever-after novel.

Although I know that I would make a much better teacher now than I was then, that opportunity has passed for me. I believe my experience was worth what I lost, but I wish I had taken a gentler, less destructive way. Mark tells me that Troy and I were doomed from the start, and he is probably right. Maybe in ten years I will have some perspective, will be able to see past the remorse. Right now I still spend too much time thinking about my losses to be truly healthy. I am too grateful for any friends that come my way, and I do not get close to men often; I am still hurt from the rejection of my friends and from Troy's infidelity and lies. I hold on to the idea that there is value in knowing myself better, in being able to understand others' experiences. I know how much strength it has taken to rebuild my life, and I had advantages—a supportive family, a good education, a few dedicated friends—so I was lucky.

Some days I can't stop crying. It's OK. Instead of expecting perfection, I have a code with Juli to indicate our emotional and mental states. "49/51," we say on the phone to each other. As long as fifty-one percent of our lives at the moment is good, we are making progress.